If GOD Is In Control, Why Do I Have a Headache?

Bible Lessons for a Woman's Total Health

Debbie Taylor Williams

new
hope
PUBLISHERS

Birmingham, Alabama

This book is not intended to provide medical advice or to take the place of medical advice and treatment from your personal doctor. Readers are advised to consult their own doctors or other qualified health professionals regarding the treatment of their medical problems. Neither the publisher nor the author is responsible to any person reading or following the information in this study.

New Hope® Publishers
P. O. Box 12065
Birmingham, AL 35202-2065
www.newhopepublishers.com

Library of Congress Cataloging-in-Publication Data

All Scripture quotations, unless otherwise indicated, are taken from the New American Standard Bible®, Copyright © 1960, 1962, 1963, 1968, 1971, 1972, 1973, 1975, 1977, 1995 by The Lockman Foundation. Used by permission.

Scripture quotations marked (KJV) are taken from The Holy Bible, King James Version.

Scripture quotations marked (NASB) are taken from the New American Standard Bible®, Copyright © 1960, 1962, 1963, 1968, 1971, 1972, 1973, 1975, 1977, 1995 by The Lockman Foundation. Used by permission.

ISBN: 1-56309-819-9

N044115 • 0804 • 6M1

Dedication

To the Lord Jesus Christ, our Savior and Redeemer,
Creator of our body, soul and spirit

"Or do you not know that your body is a temple of the
Holy Spirit who is in you, whom you have from God, and that
you are not your own? For you have been bought with a price:
therefore glorify God in your body."
—1 Corinthians 6:19–20

Table of Contents

Acknowledgments

A special thank you to the following people. You are each dear to me.

Keith, my precious husband, who provides daily encouragement and an abundance of love and prayers. Taylor and Lauren, our children, who encourage me with their prayers and calls. My sisters, Linda McConnico and Vicki Goad, whose prayers and insights are invaluable to me. Grace Williams, my mother-in-law, who prays for me.

Cynthia Itschner, for her love, insight, and help. She is a friend extraordinaire!

Debbie Ridout, for her consistent input and prayers through the years.

Pam Kanaly, whose life is an inspiration and example to me.

Pam Couch and JoAnn Dealey, friends who walk with God and love unconditionally.

Linda Schmidt, the greatest secretary in the world!

Susan Atkinson, Linda Bauman, Jean St.Clair, Martha Lou Cody, Anna Lea Donaldson, Barbara Duke, Jo Ann Hintze, Jane Longmire, Barbara Reid, Kathleen Reeves, Dorice Watts, and the class at Women's Bible Study.

Dr. John Petty, for reviewing the study and who opens his heart and church to the women of our community.

Dr. Kelly Pelton, for her input on the medical portion of the study.

Kathy Andrews, Gail Sears, Patty Russel, and Sheryl Whitworth, for their help and commitment to physical fitness and health.

Introduction

God cares about our physical struggles.

One morning as I lay in bed, God awakened me with a realization. He made it clear to me that if He was going to use me for the works He set before me, I needed to change the way I cared for my body, His temple. Rather than deprive myself of sleep, I needed to rest my body. Rather than eating carelessly, I needed to be conscious about eating the whole foods He created. Rather than neglecting my body, I needed to discipline my body. I began to realize that the physical must have attention, as well as the spiritual. *If God Is In Control, Why Do I Have a Headache?* addresses the physical as well as the spiritual trappings that can enslave a woman. It challenges her to break the bonds and live the disciplined life God designed for us.

Why should God care about our physical nature, when it is our soul that will live on with Him in eternity? The answer is found in Romans 12:1: "Present your bodies a living and holy sacrifice, acceptable to God, which is your spiritual service of worship." It is through our bodies that we serve God in this present generation.

Jesus gave His body as a living and holy sacrifice. He could have just said, "I'm praying for you," and remained in heaven! But He did more. He denied His body. He ministered through His body. It was His body that was scourged by His enemies. His body housed His Spirit, and the believer's body houses God's Spirit.

It was Christ's body that Satan tempted in an effort to thwart God's purposes. Satan tempts our bodies to thwart us from walking in the good works God has prepared for us to walk in.

Satan tempted Eve's body. Her physical, emotional, and spiritual fall came through something as simple as giving in to a certain food.

Satan's scheme to divert women from God's best has not changed. For example, his method of using food to debilitate, distract, and destroy is still intact. Is it any wonder that so many of us struggle with health and nutrition-related problems?

God cares about our bodies. We are fearfully and wonderfully made. It is through our bodies that the Spirit is animated. It is through our bodies that we point people to God, glorifying Him, or through our bodies that we suffer defeat, disease, and enslavements.

Though the Christian has no control over some diseases or physical problems, there are many choices that a woman can make to stand against the schemes of Satan and be God's best physically, emotionally, and spiritually. This study will take you through a close examination of God's care and concern for our bodies. We will see evidence of what God can do with a woman who submits her body to Him. You will be encouraged and challenged as you consider ways God wants to use your body to release His power through you.

Finally, we will consider if we are being faithful to "present [our] bodies a living and holy sacrifice, acceptable to God."

We will answer the following questions in our study:
• What does it mean to offer my body as a living sacrifice?
• How can rest, water, exercise, and nutrition affect my relationship with God and others?
• What are some practical steps I can take to make my body more fit for God's kingdom use?

If you have been struggling with health or physical issues, you are not alone. If you feel that you are not doing all God wants of you, then this study is for you. If the cry of your heart is, "God, help me! I want to serve You. I want to be used of You! I want to be a vessel of Your power in this present generation," then you will be blessed. God hears the cry of our hearts!

"For we are His workmanship, created in Christ Jesus for good works, which God prepared beforehand so that we would walk in them." —Ephesians 2:10

How to Get the Most Out of This Study

If God Is In Control, Why Do I Have a Headache? is a six-week inductive Bible study that focuses on women of the Bible and health-related issues. In each week's study, the passionate love of God is seen as He intervenes for women and touches them with His love. Jesus, the great physician, cares for women today as He cared for women of the Bible. Through the study of Esther, Hannah, and others we are able to understand how God can touch our lives as He touched theirs.

This Bible study is practical. We will take a biblical look at six women of the Bible, from both the Old and New Testaments. It will be important for you to set aside time each day to read the Bible passage. The questions are designed to let God's Word speak directly to you. The benefit to you will be the direct touch of God's Word on your heart, mind, and life.

What is it like when you do not have personal time with God and then attend your discussion group? Perhaps it might be compared to someone giving you a kiss for someone else. Have you ever had that happen? Occasionally when my husband Keith cannot go with me to see our daughter who is away at college, he will say, "Give her a kiss for me." But the kiss on the cheek I give Lauren is far different from Keith being there in person. What does Lauren miss by getting Keith's kiss secondhand? She misses the warmth of his presence. She misses his bright, dancing eyes. She misses the shared jokes and caring words that are for her alone. She misses his humor. She misses his direct thoughts and input during our discussions.

Skipping personal time with God and showing up to hear what someone else has learned is a little bit like that. Get kissed by God directly by studying the Bible for yourself!

This Bible study is up close and personal. Don't want your toes stepped on? Be warned. God's Word is up close and personal. If your toes get stepped on through God's Word, be glad. That means you are getting up close and personal with God. He is whispering in your ear. We may not like what we hear at first, but we are blessed when we are held closely in the loving arms of God. Up close and personal. That's what I want. How about you?

Each week's study will offer you the following sections:

Bible Study—To enhance your walk with God and through which you will discover answers from Scripture.

Apply God's Word—To move you from an academic study to an impacting study as you consider the Scripture in light of your life.

Up Close and Personal—To help you experience intimacy with God and His call on your life to be Christ's disciple.

A Prayer Opportunity—To provide you a place to move beyond pondering God's Word to praying over His Word and what He is impressing on your heart.

Thinking It Over—To help you sum up what you have studied throughout the week. To find the golden nugget of truth and application you want to remember. This page will also serve as your discussion guide for those studying with friends. Each day, as you go through your lesson, highlight, star, or underline key points, verses, and applications that you want to remember. You will then be able to easily complete Thinking It Over by referring to what you have already highlighted.

May your intimacy with your heavenly Father deepen, as you increasingly understand His love for you. May your eyes focus on Jesus, who goes before us as our example. May you be increasingly sensitive and responsive to the upward promptings of the Holy Spirit, who indwells the believer in love and who is our gift from God, our personal Counselor, trainer, helper, and friend. May you be richly blessed as you consider God's Word in light of your heart—and body!

Debbie

Week One

Out of Control?

Day One
Out of Control?
Esther 2:1–20

How would it feel to be freed from food, to be abandoned to God?

Father, as we begin this study, would You shower Your favor and kindness upon us? Would You open new doors of insight? Would You free us from past entanglements to pure abandonment, to be women useful for Your good purposes, in this time, in this generation in which we live? Amen.

Esther spoke saving words that were heard and used by God. Perhaps there is no greater work a woman can do than speak words that can save someone from despair, heartache, and, most importantly, living apart from God eternally.

God used Esther to save the lives of the Jews during the reign of King Xerxes, known also by his Hebrew name,

Ahasuerus. I will use his Hebrew name in this study. Esther saved her husband, the king of Persia, from making a decision to annihilate the Jews. She saved people of all ages, men and women. She saved her cousin's life.

What type of woman was Esther? Was she a self-realized woman who enthroned herself in goddess worship? Was she a headstrong personality who took the bull by the horns when she saw a crisis?

Esther was none of the above. Rather, she was like many women—quiet, unpretentious, reverent. She honored others. Self-promotion was not one of her attributes. As we recount how God used Esther, we may think, "Well, no wonder God used her. She had it easy. She was married to a king and lived in a perfect kingdom." *Not exactly, as we will discover.*

God used Esther. The question for us is how. How and why did God use Esther in such a prominent, significant way? And more importantly, how could He use me? Are there any clues we can pick up on from Esther, from her life, her decisions? I believe if we will openly consider who Esther was and how she chose to live and respond to situations and people around her, we can be blessed and useful in the kingdom of God in our present age as she was in her age, in the kingdom of Persia.

Principle:
God has called each of us to live as ambassadors for Him. God has called us to speak saving words that will affect people's souls for eternity.

In this week's study, we will consider:
1. How can God use us in situations that seem out of our control?
2. How might our being a conduit of God's grace in "out-of-control times" affect our generation as Esther affected hers?

Things can seem pretty much out of control at different times in our lives. Kids get sick. Finances take a downward spiral. Parents age. Teens face hard times. And loneliness prevails in the midst of a fast-paced society.

Out of control. Ever felt that way in relation to your body, family, finances, health, work, relationships, or world situation? Think of a recent time when you felt like nothing was going the way it was supposed to.

What were you feeling?

What did you do?

The out-of-control syndrome respects no one. That nasty little bug can attack no matter where you are, how much money you have, or what position you are in. Like a sneaky bee that circles about you when you are enjoying the beauty of a flower, so circumstances can take an odd turn. A person can set us off, or a crisis can happen, and there is a sting, a burn, or unrest.

Esther was a woman who knew what it was like to experience situations and circumstances beyond her control. **Read and record the out-of-control circumstances in her life.**

Esther 2:5–7

Esther 2:8

Esther 2:9

Esther 2:10

Esther 2:12

Where Is Susa? The mounds that were once Susa are located about 150 miles north of the Persian Gulf in southwestern Iran—an area known today as Khuzistan.

Esther 2:14, 16

Esther found herself in numerous situations that she did not ask for, nor would she have wanted. She was an orphan. She was an exile from Jerusalem. She was a captive. And although she was raised by a cousin who obviously loved and cared for her, as a young lady she was taken into custody at the citadel in Susa. In custody, she was groomed for the bedroom of the king.

What a life! What a situation to find yourself in! The young lady could have stuffed or starved herself, stormed out of the house, slammed the door behind her, and said, "I'm not going." She could have given in to depression, she could have been the most selfish one in the harem, could have, could have, could have . . . but she did not.

What excuses do we make for our behavior because of circumstances we find ourselves in? What bad choices do we make but console ourselves that "we do not have an easy life"? How might we fall short of the glory God intends for us by acting like a non-Christian in our responses to life? What can we learn from Esther when we are in situations out of our control?

As we continue reading about Esther, we pick up several hints about this young lady. We learn about her character by the choices she made. Up to this point, we have been given no indication of Esther's response to life. But in the trial of her custody, in the shame that a young Jewish lady would have felt by being groomed in a harem, we see inside the character of Esther.

What positive traits do you find about Esther from the following verses?

Esther 2:9

Esther 2:10–11

Esther 2:12–15

Esther 2:16–17

Esther 2:18

Esther 2:19–20

"The king loved Esther more than all the women" (Esther 2:17); yet in Esther 2:19 we find him gathering more virgins to his harem. Once again, Esther learned to face a situation out of her control . . . she was forced to share her husband with other women—younger and perhaps more beautiful than she.

How did Esther respond? Angrily? Rebelliously? Did she decide to defy all authority as the former Queen Vashti had done? Did she say, "Enough of this! I've tried to be a good person, but where has it gotten me?" Did she throw in the towel, raise her fist, and blame God?

Apply God's Word

1. As you think about Esther's life, think also about your life. Record some circumstances that you did not ask for, perhaps had no control over, yet faced or still face.

2. What excuses might you have made or do you still make for your response to those situations?

Up Close and Personal

1. How have you responded to the bad situations life has thrown you?

Though none of us might blame Esther if she had responded in some of the ways listed above, that is not how she responded. She did not let her mind dwell in the land of "what ifs" or the "woe is me" doldrums. That is the beauty of being a follower of God! He offers the Christian another dwelling place, a place where neither man nor beast can invade. He offers us the sanctity of a quiet place with Him where we can focus our mind, emotion, and will.

It is the outcome of Esther's choice, of her choosing the best out of what God had for her rather than dwelling on the worst life offered, that is recorded in the annals of time. It can be that way for us also. We can each make a choice today, right now, to review what has happened in our past, but rather than dwell in the past, we can move on with God. Moving on and dwelling in the hallways of intimacy with God does not discount past wrongs. It does mean moving forward and dwelling in the freedom of each new day in trust and intimacy with God.

2. What do you need to move from?

3. What do you need to move forward to and dwell on now, in this present time of your life?

A Prayer Opportunity

Can you, will you choose to dwell on the intimate love of our Lord for you and the good purposes He can bring out of your life from this moment forward, even as He did for Esther in

My character is seen by the choices I make.

each new situation in which she found herself? Record your prayer to God, asking Him to help you be like Esther, a believer who sees and chooses the best, dwelling on God's purpose in each situation.

Day Two

Choose You This Day
Esther 2:21–23

Lord God, Help us be sensitive to Your will, to Your good purposes for our lives. Help us to not hold on to past grudges, habits, or hindrances in our lives, but rather, move on to dwell in the goodness of all You offer and would have us to be. In Your arms of love we pray. Amen.

As I looked up a word in the dictionary this morning, I was amazed at the variety of words that caught my eye. As I pondered the different words, I also pondered the different responses we can have to life, to our circumstances, to our choices, even down to what we eat or how we follow up on requests made of us.

As we ponder the life of Esther, we are able to learn from her choices, words, and actions. We all have choices. As Christians, we are equipped with even more choices than those who do not profess faith in Christ.

"Choose for yourselves today whom you will serve," was the command of God through Joshua to the Israelites. Joshua 24:15 remains the cry and command of God to our hearts. It is the believer's calling to choose that which is excellent in body, mind, and spirit so that we can best reflect our Lord.

Esther found herself in a situation like many others she had faced in her life—troubling, life threatening, and lonely. She had to make decisions not only in the best interest of herself, but also of others. She was in a risky place because how and what she decided would affect others. The same holds true for us today. God calls us to select the excellent way—not the way of the world, not the way that is convenient, but the way that is true and right and good.

Why are our choices so important? Because our physical,

spiritual, and emotional choices become patterns for others to follow. An abused child learns to express anger, not manage it. Couples who divorce demonstrate divorce to their children. Adults apprentice their children by their words, behaviors, and choices.

I remember images of my mother sitting on the gold couch in our living room, sipping her coffee, looking out the window, and praying. What a valuable apprenticeship she took me through without even calling attention to what she was doing! I was apprenticed in Sunday morning ritual. We got dressed for church, filled out our offering envelopes, and off we went in the car. Daddy didn't go the first 13 impressionable years of my life. Mother apprenticed me. By the quiet demonstration of her life, she apprenticed me to go to church every Sunday. She apprenticed me to marry a Christian who *would* drive me to church.

Without speaking, we teach. With or without explanations, children pick up our signals. I wish I could re-teach some of what I taught my children. I have been less than the model God would have had me be. But with each new day, God calls us to a new opportunity to model His will. We can live in and for this day. God's love is fresh and new each day, moment by moment.

In studying Esther's life, we learn valuable lessons about how she accomplished knowing and doing God's will. An important interlude is in Esther 2:21–23. It seems but a tiny tidbit of information that we do not really need to know. But as is often the case, the tiny choices and decisions we make affect a future day.

Read Esther 2:21–23.

Who learned of the plot against King Ahasuerus?
A. Bigthan
B. Teresh
C. Mordecai

When the plot was discovered, how did Mordecai respond?

In whose name did Queen Esther inform the king?
A. Hers
B. Mordecai's
C. Haman's

How did King Ahasuerus respond to the news Esther brought to him in Mordecai's name?

Find three actions he took upon hearing the news. Esther 2:23

1)

2)

3)

The little things we do. The little things we hear. Where we happen to be. What actions we take or do not take in obedience to God. They all add up. Perhaps we will never know the missed opportunities that could have been used to weave together God's purposes had we made different little choices. But we can make choices today, sensitive to the people around us and to the God we serve.

King Ahasuerus took three steps in regard to the accusation brought against two of his officials by Mordecai and Esther. First, he investigated and found that what Mordecai and Esther said was correct. Second, he hanged his enemies. Third, he recorded the event and persons involved in the Book of the Chronicles.

Though this seems an insignificant event in the grand scheme of Esther's life, it was in fact a significant event. It was significant for several reasons, but at this time, let us consider one subtle reason. Later in Esther's life, she will again go to the king and inform him that he has an enemy in his court. Esther's credibility will be affected by this parenthesis in her life.

Can we be believed? Are the comments we make about Christ's sufficiency true? Is what we say believable to the unbelieving world? Do our choices reflect God's nature?

I cannot help but think that when the statistics for divorce, gluttony, and a multitude of other ills among believers prove to be similar to those of unbelievers, the effect on the unbeliever must be, "Why should I become a Christian?" Could it be that our credibility regarding eternal salvation is weighed by the choices we make in the flesh, in our bodies, that others see?

A listening audience is gained when we prove to be authentic. Notice I did not say when we are perfect. None of us will be perfect in this lifetime. It is okay to be a pilgrim, to be a fellow struggler with our unbelieving friends and those less mature in their faith. But if the gap between our words and our actions, our bodies and our beliefs, our standards and our stands is too great, will not the name of the One we represent be compromised?

What would have happened if Mordecai had not acted in the king's best interests? We do not know anything of how Mordecai felt when they took Esther into custody in the king's harem, but we can imagine the thoughts of his soul as he prayed for her and warned her not to divulge that she was a Jew. Yet in the midst of whatever his personal feelings were, he was faithful to report the evil intents of these men against King Ahasuerus.

If we are self-driven, we will make choices for our own pleasure and convenience. If we are God-driven, we will make choices for God's purposes.

Apply God's Word

Mordecai and Esther were credible witnesses, so the king listened to them. Consider the following questions in light of your life, and then record your answers.

1. Do I fail to have an entrée with certain people because I am not a credible witness of Christ?

2. How wide is the gap between what I say about Christ and the choices I make in the flesh?

3. In what areas could I be a more credible, authentic witness for Christ?

Up Close and Personal

Rick Warren, pastor of Saddleback Church in California, coined the phrase "purpose driven" in his book *The Purpose Driven Life*. Bottom line, what purpose drives our lives? Is it to serve God? If not, we are living less than the life God would have us live. Time to get on board like Esther did!

What really drives you in the daily motions of your life? **Check the following phrases that best describe you.**

❏ Self-driven
❏ World-driven
❏ God-driven
❏ Activity-driven
❏ Work-driven
❏ Children-driven
❏ Church-driven
❏ Physically-driven
❏ Emotionally-driven
❏ Financially-driven

A Prayer Opportunity

Every day presents an opportunity to be a fully committed Christian, to live for God's purpose in our flesh, in our present situation. What is God impressing on your heart as a result of today's study? Take this moment to direct your thoughts in prayer to your heavenly Father.

Day Three

The Kingdom of God
Esther 3:1–4:14

Lord, as we examine Your Word today, challenge us to look beyond our actions to the reasons we behave as we do. Help us to desire more than anything—more than comfort, more than food, more than convenience, more than acceptance by others—to please You and to desire to live for Your kingdom. Amen.

Living as a child of the kingdom of God means living under the rule, authority, and sovereignty of God. Examine the following passages and see if you would have made the choices Esther and Mordecai did.

Read Esther 3:1–6. Esther's cousin, Mordecai, is an interesting person for us to study. First, he saves the king's life. Then he disobeys the king's command to bow to Haman, a high official in his court. Charles Ryrie, in the Ryrie Study Bible, writes, "Apparently Mordecai did not bow to Haman because Haman claimed some sort of divine honors, as did the Persian kings. As a faithful Jew, Mordecai could not give such honor (Deuteronomy 6:13–14). Haman realized that to kill only Mordecai would not solve his problem."

Read Esther 3:7–11. This is an account of the political deal Haman cut with King Ahasuerus to annihilate the Jews. The only problem is, Haman did not mention which group of people he wished to rid from the kingdom. Of course, even if he had, the king did not know Esther was a Jew.

Read Esther 3:12–15. While King Ahasuerus and Haman sat down to drink, the city was thrown into confusion. People's lives were threatened. Wickedness prevailed. Sorrow was heaped upon the lives of an already exiled people. Was

there no end to the atrocities of those in power against the weak?

All these questions and more run through our minds with every bad circumstance that we face, that our loved ones face, that our nation faces. Where is God during this time? Where are we? Are we hiding? Are we sitting down to drink? Are we in a panic? Are we numbed, unable to move? Are we in prayer, actively calling on God, expecting an answer?

Read how Mordecai and Esther responded in Esther 4:1–12. Mordecai had facts, figures, and a favor for Esther to ask the king. She let Mordecai know that she did this at the risk of her life. Mordecai sent back a forceful answer urging, practically ordering her to do as he asked.

Esther had an order of her own to give in response to the one she received from Mordecai. **Read Esther 4:15–17. Whom did she order in Esther 4:16 and what were her words to Mordecai?**

She ordered: (Check all that apply)
❏ **Her maidens**
❏ **Mordecai**
❏ **Hathach**

What Esther replied:

Two cousins are exchanging serious words. The little girl has grown up and is now a beautiful queen living in the king's palace. She is favored and pampered by attendants, and for once life is apparently fine—not only fine, but beautiful. Now her cousin asks her to lay down all she has—in fact, to risk her life.

Mordecai's words are some of the most serious words ever spoken. His counsel is not only for his little Jewish cousin he raised but also for the queen in the palace. They are words for all people, for all time. They are words for us. Recall the famous last question Mordecai posed to Esther from Esther 4:13–14— "Who knows whether you have not attained royalty for such a time as this?" That question may often be asked of us as well.

Who knows whether you have not attained sobriety for such a time as this?

Who knows whether you have not attained your professional position for such a time as this?

Who knows whether you have not attained a lowly position for such a time as this?

Who knows whether you have not found yourself unemployed for such a time as this?

Who knows whether you have not attained wealth or poverty or motherhood or singleness—you fill in the blank—for such a time as this?

Who knows whether you have not attained being a priest and ambassador of Christ for such a time as this, in your generation, in your home, in your marriage, in your church, in your society, with your group of friends?

Principle:
We are called to be God's ambassadors
wherever we are, in whatever position or situation
we find ourselves.

The distinction between the great person and the forgotten person is what they do in the time and place where they are, not where they wish they were. To belittle our significance in God's kingdom purpose because our daily lives seem insignificant in the great scheme of eternity, or perhaps because we do not want to be bothered by God, is to miss the good works He created us to walk in.

I shared with you earlier about my mother. She never held a position deemed important by the world. Yet God used her significantly in my life. My goal as a child was to grow up and be a good mother just like her. There is no greater role a woman can play, in my opinion.

Apply God's Word
1. **How do you respond to bad news, to threatening news, to uncomfortable news?**

2. What can you do today through your bodily temple that may not be considered by the world as newsworthy, but in God's eyes is an act of spirituality for such a time as this?

3. If you have been guilty, as I have on many occasions, of dismissing the importance of daily choices, what could you pray and ask God for right now, in regard to your past, present, and future days?

So far, you may wonder what Esther's body or health has to do with the topic we are studying. But consider the following facts. When Mordecai asked Esther to speak to the king, he did so because she had physical access to the king. No other Jew was able to go in to him. When she explained to Mordecai that she might die if she used this access, it was her body she was risking. When she made a plan to prepare for this courageous step, she chose the spiritual discipline of fasting, and asked others to join her—her maids and all the Jews in Susa. We can talk about spiritual and moral courage, but Esther clearly showed physical courage!

When Mordecai urged Esther to consider that she had become a queen "for such a time as this," his words remind us that God has called each of us too. Our bodies are in different places, but God has a specific calling for each one of us in that place. If your son or your daughter is seeking a model for how to deal with anger, God has placed you there for a reason. If your coworker is desperate for guidance, God may have put you there "for such a time as this."

When we are present in these crisis situations, God has a body to work through. God in the flesh is Christ in you, the hope of glory in this present age in which we live. As God used Esther to deliver the Jews, now God is using you to impact others, through the body of flesh He has given you and in which He dwells.

> ## Principle:
> God has designed our bodies for His purpose and
> His glory wherever He has placed us.

God has given a strong body to some people, like David Robinson, that they may glorify Him in the sports arena. Others, like Joni Eareckson Tada, glorify God and influence others for Christ through their physical challenges. Still others glorify God in their body by gracing a stage or being used in a social or political arena, or by rocking a baby and teaching little ones about Jesus. Short, tall, skinny, full-bodied, beautiful, or common, God uses each according to His purpose as we maintain and offer our bodies for His use, as living and holy sacrifices, acceptable unto Him.

Up Close and Personal

1. How powerful a witness am I of God dwelling in my body of flesh?

God in the flesh is Christ in you, the hope of glory, in this present age in which we live.

2. Am I willing to learn how God can use my body, my presence, and my choices as His authentic witness today? If so, how?

3. Is my body acceptable unto God? Am I energetic, rested, and ready to serve God's purposes each day?
   ❏ Yes
   ❏ No

   Or am I sluggish, distracted from service by my own preoccupations or slothfulness?
   ❏ Yes
   ❏ No

4. Do I offer my body daily to God's service?
❑ Yes
❑ No

Or am I selfish with where I place my body and go each day?
❑ Yes
❑ No

5. Am I disciplining my body and making it my slave, as Paul described in 1 Corinthians 9:24–27?
❑ Yes
❑ No

Or am I soft, undisciplined—enslaved to my body and fleshly desires?
❑ Yes
❑ No

These and many other questions point us to the need to consider the importance of our body and our health in relation to the Holy Spirit within. Jesus Christ healed women's bodies. With their restored bodies and spirits they served Him and God's purposes. God's command is that we love God with all our heart, soul, mind, and strength, and love our neighbor as our self. To be obedient to God's command we need to be responsible in body, mind, and spirit.

The fact is, God used Esther's beauty, her body, to find favor with those she was around, and to find rank in the kingdom of earth so that the will of heaven might be accomplished through her. The fact is, God used Jesus' body on the cross to accomplish our salvation. The fact is, God still desires to use the believer's body, which He indwells for His kingdom purposes.

Principle:
In God's eyes, we are created for but one purpose, and that is to glorify Him.

Anything that sets us on a course physically, spiritually, or emotionally that is not glorifying to God is a distortion of the life He meant us to live. Today the Christian has a great opportunity to be authentic, to be credible. May we do so in our spirit and flesh as we serve God not just with our mind and words, but also by our choices and actions in the flesh! May we glorify God in our bodies!

A Prayer Opportunity

What is God impressing on your heart as a result of today's study? Take this moment to direct your thoughts in prayer to your heavenly Father.

Day Four

The Three-Day Fast

Released for God's Purposes
Esther 4:15–17

Lord, help us be honest in our assessment of ourselves. Help us look inwardly and upwardly to You and consider if we are released for Your purposes in our life. If we are living for our own purpose, for our own will, in body, soul, or spirit, teach us the keys to being released unto You. Amen.

Esther served God's purposes in her body as she lived under His reign and authority, trusting His sovereignty in her life. How many of us can say that about our current situation? I am not speaking of church attendance. Jesus' challenges to His disciples never carried such a light commitment. His meaning of discipleship was always clear. Discipleship was costly. Discipleship was definitive. **Record Christ's definition of discipleship from His words in Matthew 10.**

Matthew 10:24

Matthew 10:27

Matthew 10:28

Matthew 10:32–33

Matthew 10:37

Matthew 10:38

Matthew 10:39

From additional Scriptures, we know that disciples were not perfect men and women, but they did understand the call of God on their life. They did understand and experience what commitment to Christ cost. Do we? Are we truly believers, truly disciples, who have taken up our cross and are following after Jesus? These are the words of our Lord, recorded in Matthew 10:38— "And he who does not take his cross and follow after Me is not worthy of Me."

Hard times call for hard choices. So do easy times. In the easy as well as the hard, do we choose Christ? Do we live under His power, authority, and reign? Is Christ's reign evident by our actions and speech, by our passions and time commitments, by the way we raise our children, and relate to our husbands and other family members? Are we following after Christ, going the way of a believer, seeking the unsaved to bring into the kingdom of God? Or are we following our own way, neglecting the things of God unless they're convenient?

We can learn a lot from Esther. We learn by observing how she responded to life's situations. We learn she chose to be better, not bitter, when her parents died. We learn she was pleasant, not pouting, when in custody. She was astute, not arrogant, when it was time for her to go to the king. She was submissive, yet not a pushover, when Mordecai ordered her to plead for the Jews' lives.

A word that describes Esther is repeated in Esther 2:9, 2:15, and 2:17. That word is "favor." Esther is described as a

> Disciples are not perfect men and women, but they do understand the call of God on their lives.

pleasant, kind person who found favor in the eyes of all. Though God is not mentioned in the Book of Esther, we cannot avoid the fact that her whole life was wrapped up in Him. She was in exile because she was a Jew who believed in the one true God. In the passage we are now studying, she is called on to confess her faith in the one true God and go to the king at risk of her own life, to implore that he spare her race.

In Esther 4:15–17, we learn how Esther responds to the greatest challenge and test she has yet faced. As she prepares to face the king, she asks others to fast with her.

Who is called on to fast? Check all that apply.
❑ **Esther**
❑ **The whole harem**
❑ **Esther's maidens**
❑ **Mordecai**
❑ **All the Jews in Susa**

How long were they to fast?
A. One day
B. Two days
C. Three days

Serious times are often marked in Scripture by a call to a fast. In our present day, fasts are seldom heard of. Perhaps the most common fast heard of is when a person is told to fast before a medical test or laboratory work. Then it is usually only for a period of hours. Some Christians fast from a particular drink or food, such as coffee or chocolate, during the Lenten season.

In the Bible, fasting is not an uncommon but rather a common discipline. Jesus said, "*When* you fast," not "*If* you fast" (Matthew 6:16). When the disciples asked why they could not cast demons out of a man's son, Jesus responded, "But this kind does not go out except by prayer and fasting" (Matthew 17:21).

Why is fasting not a common discipline in our day? The reason may be because we are not practiced in the spiritual disciplines. Rather than read our Bibles, we rely on a preacher to teach or inspire us. Rather than deny our body foods we crave and which in fact may be bad for our health, we indulge the flesh. Unfortunately, the neglect of the discipline of fasting unto God has cost us, evidenced by spiritually impoverished believers who lack self-control and power.

Esther used the fast to prepare her mind, body, and spirit for the work God called her to do. Rather than go into a nervous frenzy, raid the king's refrigerator, and call the Jews into a panic, she introduced a calming force and a submissive spirit into the events that were to take place.

Can we learn from her? Could it be that many of us do not sense God speaking or do not have God's empowerment in our lives because we neglect the discipline of fasting? Some people contend that fasting is not good for the body, but how would they respond to the fact that Jesus fasted? Would the perfect Son of God do something harmful to His body, something that would hurt the temple of God? Hardly, for that would be sin, and Jesus committed no sin. Granted, not all persons can fast, due to health reasons or medications they are taking. Certainly any person under medical care who is considering fasting should first seek the advice of their physician. But there are many of us who can fast, and for whom it would be appropriate and powerful.

Consider the role of fasting throughout the Bible:
• Jesus fasted (Matthew 4:2).
• Anna fasted (Luke 2:36–37).
• Moses fasted (Exodus 34:28; Deuteronomy 9:9, 18).
• Paul fasted (Acts 9:9).
• Nehemiah fasted (Nehemiah 1:4)
• Ezra fasted (Ezra 8:21–23).
• Barnabas and Simeon fasted (Acts 13:1–2).
• Daniel fasted (Daniel 9:3).
• And others . . .

Record what the following Scriptures say about fasting.

Matthew 6:16

Matthew 9:15

Acts 13:2–3

Acts 14:23

Serious times are often marked in Scripture by a call to a fast.

Andrew Murray, in his book *With Christ in the School of Prayer*, explains, "Fasting helps to express, to deepen, and to confirm the resolution that we are ready to sacrifice anything, to sacrifice ourselves to attain what we seek for the kingdom of God." Could the purpose of fasting be better stated?

Esther was at a point of sacrifice and resolution. The fast she partook of empowered her to do the work God had set before her. Do we have such resolve to serve God in our body?

Apply God's Word
Consider the following.

1. Have I ever fasted to express, to deepen, and to confirm the resolution that I am ready to sacrifice anything, including myself, to attain what I seek for the kingdom of God?
❑ Yes
❑ No

2. Have I ever fasted to loosen sin's grip or to be loosed from an enslavement of the flesh?
❑ Yes
❑ No

3. Have I ever fasted to become a more available vessel for God?
❑ Yes
❑ No

Up Close and Personal
1. What sin do I need to be loosed from?

2. In what way do I need to be a more available vessel for God?

A Prayer Opportunity

What is God impressing on your heart as a result of today's study? Take this moment to direct your thoughts in prayer to your heavenly Father.

For information on the spiritual, physical, and emotional benefits of fasting, I recommend *God's Chosen Fast: A Spiritual and Physical Guide to Fasting* by Arthur Wallis.

Day Five
Following God's Timing
Esther 5:1–6:14

Father, as we see how You placed Esther in a place and time to be used of You, so we seek to be used of You. In the time we are in right now, in the place where we are, use us! May we sacrifice all to You. In Your name we pray. Amen.

Read Esther 5:1–4. We can almost taste the moment as Esther dons her royal clothes. But wait! What happened during the interlude of her three-day fast? We can only imagine, but may I suggest, from fasts I have been blessed by, that the teachings and empowerment of God upon her were abundant. God's calling and purpose for our life becomes more clear when we fast unto Him. Esther would have gone into the king with great resolve, with great peace. If she died, she died.

Notice King Ahasuerus' response. What was it? Check all that are true.
❏ He called the guards to take her away.
❏ He extended the golden scepter to her.
❏ He saw her in favor.
❏ He allowed her to come near.
❏ He allowed her to touch the top of the golden scepter.
❏ He offered up to half of his kingdom to her.

Why did Esther not say, "Great! I'd like the half that are the Jews!" Why did she invite him to a banquet? Was it because

she was starving after her fast and felt she could think more clearly if she had a good meal? Was she thinking, "I just don't have the strength to go through with this"? Perhaps. Perhaps not. Perhaps the Spirit of God was leading her!

What might she have been blessed to experience in light of Matthew 10:19–20, 27?

Continue reading Esther 5:5–8. What happened? Did Esther chicken out at banquet number one? Did she lose her nerve? Was she having such a good time she questioned if she should even risk mentioning her mission? We do not know the details of Esther's waiting, but what a glorious outcome her waiting brought! **Read Esther 5:9–14** to get a picture of what was happening in the interlude of one day's wait.

Haman was angry! Though he had all that he desired in terms of position, wealth, and the favor of the king, he could not stand that Mordecai did not tremble before him or honor him.

Haman's friends and wife had an easy solution. What was it? Read Esther 5:14.

Here we see a marked contrast between the spiritual woman and the worldly woman. Worldliness thinks on her own and draws her own conclusions based on pride, convenience, and ease. Spirituality draws on God, seeks His perspective, and sacrifices self up to the service of the One who created us.

Principle:
**God calls us to be spiritual people
in our bodies of flesh.**

Are we worldly or spiritual in everyday life? Esther 6 brings a great shift in the scene. **Read in Esther 6:1–5 what happened**

to King Ahasuerus during the night.
Check all that apply.
❏ He had a dream about Mordecai.
❏ He could not sleep.
❏ He had the book of records, the chronicles, read to him.
❏ He discovered he had never honored Mordecai, who had
   saved his life.

We never know how yesterday's gesture of kindness will affect tomorrow. In this case, we are thankful that Mordecai reported the plot against the king's life. We are also glad that Esther, sensitive to God's timing, waited with her request!

The story at this point could not be scripted with more plot twists. Haman, who has desired nothing more than to be honored by Mordecai, is now honoring Mordecai, leading the horse that Mordecai sits upon.

Can you imagine the thrill of the Jews in Susa? They had not been privy to what was going on in God's sovereign plan, but now they see Mordecai seated upon the king's horse and robed in honor. Can you imagine how they praised God? Can you imagine the continued prayers that flowed from their hearts as they received word that tonight Esther would make her request! Their fasting unto God, seeking His help for that which was beyond their control, had moved mountains. A three-day fast is not such a huge sacrifice in order for one to taste freedom and God's empowerment!

As we draw close to the end of Esther's role in this scenario, continue reading in Esther 7:1–6. Notice her meekness in verse 4 and her boldness in verse 6.

How did Esther exude humbleness in Esther 7:4?

How did Esther exude boldness in Esther 7:6?

Keep reading Esther 7:7–10. It only gets better! Notice how Harbonah was only too ready to offer the gallows prepared

for Mordecai to be used for Haman. Haman's true nature was found out because of Esther, who waited her time, sought God's will through fasting, and submitted her life to serve God's purpose.

Esther did not know the end of the story at any point, just as we do not know what our next moment will bring. If we were to take any one segment of her life, we can see how she could have made human choices apart from God. She could have indulged in despair. Esther could have turned to physical and emotional comforts such as food and drink, rather than fast. She could have refused when God wanted to use her as a godly influence for her nation. She could have made those choices, but she chose God's best.

God has designed women to be uniquely used for His glory. Women hold opportunities as helpmates to husbands and as mothers, aunts, teachers to children, caregivers, employees, employers, volunteers, and spiritual neighbors to those around us. Are we on board with God or are we dead weight?

> ## Principle:
> ### God uses our bodies to serve Him.

A submitted will in a body enslaved to sin is an unhealthy temple. The spirit may be willing, but if the flesh is weak we must cry to God and perhaps fast unto Him for deliverance, even as Esther did.

Our bodies are wonderfully made. God made them in His image. We are given eyes to see those around us. We are given ears to hear their cry. We are given hands with which to serve. With our feet we can walk in the good works God prepared for us and that give meaning and purpose to our life. We are created to function at a high energy level. We are given muscles to be toned, minds to be quickened, and understanding by which we can commune with God.

In recent years fast foods, preservatives, additives, fried foods, and foods high in sugar, salt, and fat have taken their toll on the human body, and they cost us—physically, emotionally, and spiritually. Lack of physical exercise and drinks

substituted for water have caused the general populace to encounter health problems. Running our gas tank on low octane fuel rather than the premium whole foods God created has caused havoc in our internal and external systems. This problem is now recognized by not only our physicians, but by the general public. I encourage you to consider your health from God's perspective.

For the Christian, care of the body goes beyond a national call to fitness or a sensual call to sexiness. It is a call for Christians to reach for God's highest in their lives.

If you are addicted to certain foods or are overeating, weighted with not only pounds but also guilt about any enslavement, I encourage you to seek information about how foods and drinks can affect your body, mind, moods, and actions.

Following is an excerpt from Elizabeth Somer's book *Food and Mood*. Perhaps you will discover as I did that sometimes what may seem to be a spiritual dilemma or lack of self-control in an area of indulgence is actually a physical craving related to a nutritional need. By better stewardship of our bodies, the incorporation of healthy choices, and yes, perhaps even fasting unto God, we can find freedom from enslavements that hinder our walk, worship, and work for God's best purposes in our lives.

> *It now appears that what we eat can affect whether we are happy, sad, irritable, moody, alert, calm, or sleepy. Some nutrients in food might improve memory, give a boost of energy, or satisfy an otherwise insatiable appetite. Most people understand that what they eat affects their physical health. So it makes sense that diet has just as great an impact on how we feel, think, act, and sleep.*

God used Esther—an orphan, an exile, taken into custody in a harem, separated from the only family she had, set apart in a kingdom that was not her own. God wants to use us, set apart in this earthly kingdom that is not ours, while we await our true kingdom in heaven. God wants to use us. Are we willing? Are we wise as Esther was to look toward God's higher purposes for her life?

Apply God's Word

1. How often, how much does the outpouring of your soul result in the overflow of praise because you are a part of the spiritual workings of God?

2. Who do you most identify with in the Book of Esther?

Up Close and Personal

Esther could have turned to physical and emotional comforts such as food and drink, rather than fasting. She could have refused how God wanted to use her in her family and nation as a godly influence. She could have, but she did not. She chose God's best instead.

1. Are you living your life unto God or unto self?

2. Are you indulging in despair, depression, food, or some other comfort rather than fasting unto God when trouble or serious situations come close to home?

3. How are you challenged by Esther?

A Prayer Opportunity

What is God impressing on your heart as a result of today's study? Take this moment to direct your thoughts in prayer to your heavenly Father.

Week One
Thinking It Over

Please look back over your lesson and prayerfully complete the following.

1. What was most meaningful to you in your study of Esther from:

Day 1:

Day 2:

Day 3:

Day 4:

Day 5:

2. How did God convict, stir, or prompt your heart and mind through Esther's life?

3. God used prayer and fasting in Esther's life. How might God want to use you as He did Esther, as a conduit of His grace in what appears to be a situation beyond your control?

4. What response to His Word might God want you to make as a result of studying about Esther?

5. What "golden nugget" of truth do you want to remember?

6. What verse do you want to remember from this week's study?

7. What is the prayerful cry of your heart in relation to this week's study?

If God Is In Control, Why Do I Have a Headache?

Day One
Peter's Mother-In-Law
Luke 4:31–39

In times of sickness, in times of health, how do we respond to illness and to others around us?

Father, may we be humble enough to recognize that our lives are not our own. If it is Your desire that our poor health or physical condition not be restored but rather be a tool for Your glory, then give us grace to meet each day. If it is Your will, we pray for healing and in that, give You all praise and glory. Amen.

As I knelt and prayed one morning, my thoughts turned to a headache that had crept up. The past few days, in fact weeks, had been fast paced as preparations stepped up for our annual Women of Passion and Purpose Conference.

God had been faithful to provide for every detail. He had shown His powerful hand in the Friday night outdoor concert preparations and the Saturday conference sessions. All were enthused and expectant. Many details remained to be taken care of, and for these details, I prayed. That's when it dawned on me that I had a headache!

I could not help but laugh. "Why should I have a headache, God, if You are in control?" I prayed. The question continued to penetrate my thoughts and prayer time. If God was in control of the event, if it was His idea and He was bringing it to pass, why should I, at this point, take on undue stress? It did not make sense, and I am glad He reminded me that He was in control, so I did not need a headache!

I continued to think on the question, however. Do we really believe God is in control? Is God really in control? Or do we attempt to control events, people's lives, and circumstances in our own flesh? Do we ever attempt to control events God never intended we control?

God is good. He did not create Eve with a headache or any other physical suffering. But in humanity's fallen condition, suffering pain is not uncommon. Many live with chronic pain. In fact, according to a CBS News/*Prevention* magazine poll, three out of four Americans say they suffer from some type of pain.

There are numerous reasons for pain, some of which we have no control over. But in some cases, there are actions we can take to avoid or stave off certain painful physical conditions.

As stated in the introduction, God looks with compassion upon us when we are hurting or physically suffering pain. Throughout the Bible, we see Jesus' compassion for those who suffered.

In this week's study we will answer the following questions:
1. How does my health affect my relationship with God?
2. How does my physical condition affect my relationship with others?
3. What does God expect of me in regard to the stewardship of my body?

Today we begin our study of Peter's mother-in-law with the background passage Luke 4:31–37. **Read Luke 4:31–37, then** answer the following questions regarding Jesus' dramatic healing of the possessed man.

What city were Jesus and His disciples in?
A. Capricorn
B. Calisto
C. Capernaum

What was Jesus doing on this particular day?
A. Fishing
B. Teaching
C. Walking on water

Who was in the synagogue as Jesus taught?
A. Jews
B. A demoniac

What kind of fellowship did they experience on that particular Sabbath?
A. Sweet
B. Disrupted

How was the teaching of Jesus disrupted?

What does the word "us" spoken by the demoniac imply when he says "Let us alone!"?

What did the demon suppose Jesus had come to do?

Why is the demon's fear valid? John 12:31

In John 16:11, Jesus states the condition of Satan. What is it?
A. He has been judged.
B. He will be judged.

Jesus stated that judgment was on the world, that the ruler of this world would be cast out, and that Satan, the ruler, had already been judged. **How does 1 John 3:8b, "The Son of God**

appeared for this purpose, to destroy the works of the devil," fit with what Jesus did in Luke 4:31–35?

The final verses in our background passage today state the response of those who witnessed Jesus healing the man. **How did they respond? Check all that apply.**
❏ **They were amazed.**
❏ **They were angry.**

What were they curious about?
❏ **How a man with an unclean spirit sneaked into the synagogue.**
❏ **Jesus' message.**

We can only hope and pray that God's work in us would make people wonder about our message of the good news of Jesus Christ. Jesus looked on people's physical conditions and healed them. Jesus looked on people's spiritual condition and healed them. He still does.

> ### Principle:
> **We can join Jesus in His work. We can join His war against sin and the effects of sin on our body, soul, and spirit.**

Apply God's Word

Jesus referred to Satan as the ruler of this world on numerous occasions. **How often do you contemplate that there is an invisible war between God and the devil, whom Jesus refers as "the ruler of this world"?**

How active are you in standing firm with Jesus against anything siding with Christ's enemy?

Satan, the ruler of this world, wants to destroy my body if he can't have my soul.

Up Close and Personal

Jesus looked on others' physical conditions with compassion. If Jesus had concern for people's physical conditions in biblical days, do you feel He is still concerned today?

❑ Yes
❑ No

To what degree do you think His concern extends to you?

How are you cooperating with Jesus in regard to your physical health?

❑ I'm not!
❑ I eat healthy foods.
❑ I keep my body fit by exercising regularly.

In Luke 4:31–37, we find that Jesus has come and is destroying the works of the destroyer. The ruler of this world destroys physical, emotional, and spiritual health. Jesus restores. May you be blessed as you ponder Jesus' eyes of compassion on you!

A Prayer Opportunity

Write a prayer to God, as you contemplate your physical, emotional, and spiritual health. How is God working to restore or perfect you?

Day Two

Jesus Cares About You

Luke 4:37–39

Lord, how we thank You for the awakening that Your eyes of compassion are not just for extreme cases of illness, but for a mother-in-law with a fever. How grateful we are, how humbled we are as we consider that Your eyes are upon us. When we consider that You see our physical condition, we ask You to teach and guide us if we have a habit that is destroying our health, our effectiveness for You. In Your name we pray, Amen.

Often we might be prone to read the Scriptures from a third party position. We might read and speculate rather than contemplate what God's Word means for us. We might be guilty of saying, "That was for *then*. That was for *them*."

When we take God's words seriously, though, and for us, He gives us a heart to better understand His Word. The passage we are studying today gives insight into the heart of Jesus for all people, not just for those 2000 years ago.

In today's Scripture we find Jesus caring for one woman's health needs. **Read Luke 4:37–39. Why was Jesus' effect on people's physical condition being reported?**

We tend to spread good news. The latest diet plan may become a best seller. Books on health abound.

We gravitate to good news or even to what appears to be good news. How fantastic it would be if Christians led the way in the health field for taking care of our bodies, the temple of the Holy Spirit. Consider the opportunities one might have when asked how they managed to stay on a diet and exercise routine. What "good news" bearers we could be! Perhaps we might even gain an audience with non-believing family members, neighbors, or coworkers.

Jesus' healing and compassion are not just for extreme health needs.

Jesus got the attention of one woman. I believe He wants to get our attention, too. **Read Luke 4:38–39. After Jesus left the synagogue, where did He go?**

What was the condition of Simon's mother-in-law?

She had probably not been to the synagogue that day. Not only did she have a fever, it was high. The Scripture tells us that she was suffering. Notice the tenderness of those in the home who surrounded Peter's mother-in-law. Perhaps it was Peter or maybe his wife who approached Jesus. **What did they ask Jesus?**

That was right up Jesus' alley! He came to help us! His ultimate help is remedying our spiritual condition. But He is also concerned with our present condition, our spirits, emotions,

and bodies, for we are His instruments, the delight of His eyes and His glory.

Jesus stood over her and rebuked the fever. Can you imagine lying in bed, suffering with a high fever, and then rousing to see Jesus Christ standing over you? The Great Physician is on the scene and He is the Restorer!

Granted, it is not always God's will to bring healing in our lifetime on earth. Sometimes suffering is not alleviated in this age, but rather in the age to come. However, we can still pray for health and healing while accepting God's ultimate will.

When the Scripture said that Jesus rebuked the fever, the word *rebuke* in the Greek language means "censure" or "admonish, forbid." How nice it would be if Jesus forbid some of our habits or lifestyle choices that lead to poor health. But then again, the Bible does! **Fill in the following blanks.**

Proverbs 23:20— "Do not be with heavy _____ of _____; or with _____ eaters of meat."

1 Corinthians 10:31— "Whether, then, you _____ or _____ or whatever you do, do all to the glory of God."

1 Corinthians 9:27— "But I _____ my body and make it my _____, so that, after I have preached to others, I myself will not be disqualified."

1 Corinthians 6:12 reminds us, "All things are lawful for me, but not all things are profitable. All things are lawful for me, but I will not be mastered by anything."

Principle:
God has commands regarding food, drink, and even how we respond to stress because He cares about our physical condition.

Luke 4:39 records that Jesus rebuked the fever. Only in recent years have we begun to understand why Jesus "forbids" or

"rebukes" stress, worrying, gluttony, drunkenness, self-indulgence, laziness, bitterness, and other harmful behaviors. They are ailments of the body and soul, as Peter's mother-in-law's fever was. They are symptoms of internal imbalances.

God created our bodies wonderfully. His commands that forbid certain activities or extremes and His commands instructing us in the right ways are for our health, protection, and fulfillment.

Take God's Word on the subject of worry, for instance. What does Jesus say? **Write out the following verse inserting your name in it. Matthew 6:25**

What point of logic and reason does Jesus make in the next verse, Matthew 6:27?

How does Jesus emphasize God's compassion and love for you, while at the same time challenging you to greater faith?

Matthew 6:34 "Do not _____ **about tomorrow; for tomorrow will take care of itself. Each day has enough** _____ **of its own."**

If you or I were standing before Jesus with a load of worries weighing us down, making us grieve, miserable, sick at our stomach, affecting our sleep, leading us to be irritable and short tempered, what do you think He would do, knowing that our symptoms had an internal root?

I believe Jesus would treat the tension in the shoulders, heal the upset stomach, and forbid the worrisome attitude and pattern of thinking that produced the physical symptoms.

More than 2000 years after Jesus commanded us to not worry, we are learning why stress is so bad for us. Jesus rebukes worry as a response to stress for our health and best interest.

In the Matthew account, when Jesus looked at the crowd He understood their stresses, financial concerns, clothing and food needs, political pressures, and family stresses. Jesus knew the psychological and physiological harm of worry and offered a way to respond to stress.

First, what did Jesus assure the listeners of? Matthew 6:31–32

Second, what did Jesus say to do? Matthew 6:33

Jesus' compassion and concern for man is obvious. He loves us!!! Jesus does not want us to worry! He is so sincere about us not worrying and suffering the consequences of worry that He forbids it! **Record Jesus' words, inserting your name in the verse. Matthew 6:34a**

Why does Jesus, in Matthew 6:34b, say not to worry? Check all that are true.
❏ **Tomorrow will care for itself.**
❏ **Each day has enough trouble of its own.**

Stress is now known to contribute to disease. Findings by an Ohio State research group, which appeared in the *Proceedings of the National Academy of Sciences*, address the effects of stress on the body. The article, "Stress Can Make You Sick" reported, "It's no surprise that constant stress can make people sick, and now a team of researchers has figured out how." A study focused on 119 people, men and women, who were taking care of spouses with dementia. The health of the caregivers was compared with that of 106 people of similar ages who were not living under the stress of constant caregiving. Blood tests showed that a chemical called Interleukin-6 sharply increased in the blood of the stressed caregivers compared with blood of the others in the test. Previous studies have associated IL-6 with several diseases, including heart diseases, arthritis, osteoporosis, type-2 diabetes, and certain cancers.

The study also found the increase in IL-6 can linger in caregivers for as long as three years after a caregiver has ceased that role because of the spouse's death. Of the test

group, 78 spouses died during the survey. "This really makes a link to why chronic stress can actually kill people," said Janice Kiecolt-Glaser, professor of psychology and psychiatry at The Ohio State University. She explained that people under stress tend to respond by doing things that increase their levels of IL-6. For example, they may smoke or overeat; smoking raises IL-6 levels, and the chemical is secreted by fat cells. Stressed people also may not get enough exercise or sleep, she added. Exercise reduces IL-6, she said, and normal sleep helps regulate levels of the chemical.

Jesus offers an alternate way to respond to stress. When stressed, we can smoke, drink, overeat, not sleep enough, and not exercise. In so doing, the IL-6 chemical will be raised and we will become sicker. Or, we can pray, tell God our needs, and seek His kingdom rule in the situation that is causing us stress. We can eat the foods of the earth He created for our bodies, fresh vegetables and fruits and lean meats and fishes. We can exercise. We can lie down in peace, meditating on God as we lie on our bed.

If God's in control, why do I have a headache? Perhaps I have a headache because I worry and do not get enough sleep. Maybe I have a headache because I have a vitamin deficiency because of poor eating habits. Perhaps I have a headache because I have a chemical imbalance because I do not exercise. My headache may be the result of foods I eat that have preservatives or additives. Perhaps I have a headache due to muscle tension in my upper back and neck because of carrying too heavy a purse, or because of sitting too long in one position at the computer, for which a massage would be beneficial. Maybe I have some other condition and should make an appointment with a doctor.

Jesus saw the fever in Peter's mother-in-law and treated the fever and the cause. Jesus sees the stress in our lives. His desire is to help us and lead us if we will listen and obey.

Apply God's Word
How do today's Scriptures point to God's concern for you physically, spiritually, and emotionally?

Which of today's Scriptures might God want you to take to heart?

Up Close and Personal

On the basis of Jesus' care for Peter's mother-in-law, would you consider how He might be very interested in one more woman . . . you! **If Jesus rebuked or forbid any physical condition in you because of His love for you, what would it be?**

How could your compliance with Jesus be an opportunity for God's glory?

Principle:
Each of us is important to God, even as Peter's mother-in-law was.

A Prayer Opportunity

Jesus cared about one woman, her symptoms, and her health. He cares about you. Are there any physical or emotional symptoms such as irritability, lethargy, excessive dieting, or overeating that present a nutritional or health concern for you?

Is there any suffering that could be alleviated by better nutrition, attention to medication, exercise, or lifestyle changes? Are there any ways you are working against your body rather than with it for optimal health? If so, let the cry of your heart go before God. In confession, ask God for His insight, direction, and the desire to do the right things.

Day Three

Instant Messaging . . .
He Touched Her

Matthew 8:14–15

Heavenly Father, thank You that in this day of computers and instant messaging, You are present with Your message of love. Thank You that You don't "freeze up," " shut down," or "get viruses"; that You touch us in love. In Christ's name, Amen.

Lauren could not wait to get instant messaging. First, she had to educate me on what it was. "You can just talk back and forth on the computer and don't even have to wait to email. It's so much faster!" I could just imagine the hours she would then spend talking to her friends, in addition to the time she already spent on the telephone! When she went away to college, she finally got "instant messaging" and then could not wait for me to get it *so we could talk faster*. Precious dear! I have to say it was fun! Amazingly, Lauren could carry on multiple conversations with numerous people all at the same time, and not lose a beat with any of them! She had an additional way to "reach out and touch someone," as the saying goes.

Instant messaging gave an additional insight to me. It brought to my attention the relationship we have with God. Our heavenly Father is available for us to go "online" with Him any time, day or night. He is always there, even if others are talking to Him at the same time. I do not know how He does it, but neither do I understand how instant messaging works, and it does. My faith is increased by technology. I hope yours is, too!

In today's passage, we are going to see how Jesus reached out and touched one woman. We are going to discover the instant message He sent her. Most importantly we are going to explore the four ways Jesus has arranged to have an instant message relationship with us and touch our lives.

Read Matthew 8:14–15, Matthew's account of Jesus' healing Peter's mother-in-law. In compassion, Jesus looked at Peter's mother-in-law. In intimacy, He responded to the "instant message" prayer request of her family. What does

Matthew observe that is not recorded in Luke's account? Luke observed Jesus' words. Matthew observed Jesus' touch.

What kind of touch did Matthew observe? Check one.
❏ **A touch on her forehead that threw her to the ground.**
❏ **A touch on her hand after which she got up and served Him.**

The word *touch* in Greek is the word *haptomai*, and means "to attach oneself to." It is from a primary verb that means "to fasten to," specifically "to set on fire, kindle, light." *Touch* in the Greek refers to handling in such a way as to exert a modifying influence upon. It is used elsewhere in the Gospels to describe Jesus' healing touch on people.

Matthew 8:3 Jesus touched a leper.
Matthew 9:29 Jesus touched the eyes of two blind men.
Matthew 17:7 Jesus touched the disciples when they were afraid.
Mark 7:33 Jesus touched the ears of a deaf man.
Luke 7:14 Jesus touched a dead man's coffin and raised him to life.
Luke 22:51 Jesus touched the right ear of the high priest's slave.

What did Jesus feel as He looked upon sick people? Compassion. His compassion caused Him to reach out and touch them in order to exert a modifying influence on them.

Jesus still feels compassion for His children. Jesus cares when He looks on those blinded to how they are eating themselves to death. Jesus feels compassion on one with an alcohol or drug addiction. Jesus feels compassion for a person who is enslaved to an unhealthy lifestyle. Jesus has compassion for a person who looks in the mirror and thinks she is fat, who struggles with anorexia, bulimia, or obesity. Jesus cares about the diabetic. Jesus cares about a person struggling with cancer. Jesus feels for a person suffering with chronic fatigue syndrome, irritability, insomnia, and the host of other ailments that accompany our world and lifestyle. Jesus cares and desires to kindle and light a cleansing, changing fire in us. Jesus desires to exert a modifying influence on us!

Instant messaging gave an additional insight to me. It brought to my attention the relationship we have with God.

Our opportunity to receive God's instant message of love and touch on our lives is experienced through four avenues.

1. We can prayerfully send God the message that we want His help.
2. We can know His message to us through His Word.
3. Christ can touch our lives through a physician, nutritionist, preacher, family, or friend.
4. We can be sensitive to His touch through the Holy Spirit.

God has an instant message of love. God has a life-changing touch. He is reaching out to touch someone. Could it be you?

As we examine the four ways Christ reaches out and touches our lives, consider how open you are to His touch through the Holy Spirit, His Word, prayer, and His messengers. How much are you being modified into Christ's image because your heart is open to Him?

First, Peter and his family "prayed." They spoke to Jesus and asked for His help regarding their loved one's physical condition. **Find three points in Hebrews 4:14–16 regarding our relationship with Jesus.**

1.

2.

3.

What, in particular, can we pray about? Philippians 4:6

What is the result of going to our high priest and praying? Philippians 4:7

The Bible teaches us to talk to God, to pray about everything. Nothing is insignificant in God's eyes. To assume God is too busy to bother with our need is to assume God is limited in His capacity and time. God desires to touch our life. Prayer is the first key to whatever health or lifestyle issue we face and want modified for Christ's glory.

The second way we receive God's touch is through His Word. Jesus rebuked Peter's mother-in-law's fever. His Word went forth, commanding His will in compassion for her. Christ's words were meant to alter her condition.

Christ's words are meant to alter our life. The lifestyle He rebukes, we should avoid. The commandments He speaks, we should do. As we read the Bible, we are reminded of what He forbids and commands for our best interest.

An example of God's words that we should follow and that affect our health can be found in Philippians 4:8. **What does God's Word command?**

The third way our compassionate High Priest touches us is through others. God uses ministers, teachers, physicians, nutritionists, Christian friends, and family to speak to us. An example of God using a messenger to touch our lives is in Paul's writing to the Philippians. **What is Paul's message to the Philippians and to us? Philippians 4:9**

The fourth way God sends His "instant message" of love is through the Holy Spirit. This is perhaps one of the most exciting ways God communicates with us. The Holy Spirit prompts our mind and conscience according to the Word of God.

Because the Holy Spirit's touch is gentle, the believer can ignore the Holy Spirit. The believer can continue in forbidden self-indulgences and a lifestyle that contributes to poor health and, ultimately, illness. Or the believer can pray and learn to be sensitive to the Holy Spirit's promptings. The believer can learn to walk by the Spirit of God and find her life modified by God's power! **How does Galatians 5:16 encourage the believer to walk by the Holy Spirit?**

God's Word teaches us to be self-controlled, to walk by the Spirit. The more we study the Bible, the more we can sense God's touch. The more we respond to God's touch, the more we reflect our Maker.

How can we be more sensitive to the Spirit's touch? We can pray for the Holy Spirit to fill our heart, mind, and spirit, to reign in us, to use us. In prayer, we open our heart and invite God's modifying influence over us.

Principle:
Christ desires the utmost intimacy with Christians and has given to us His Spirit, through whom He communicates with us.

What does all this mean in terms of our health? Christians have a helper, comforter, mentor, guide, prompter dwelling within our very being! Christ touches us and modifies us through prayer, the Bible, others, and the Holy Spirit.

Perhaps some of us have fallen short in heeding Christ's touch regarding our bodies and health. Perhaps God has spoken to us about eating whole natural foods of the earth, but we continue to glibly eat processed, chemically-infused preserved foods. Perhaps we neglect to strengthen and exercise our body, then wonder why we are "down" or "blue" all the time. Perhaps we go to the doctor, but continue to abuse our temples or do not take prescribed medication. Perhaps we cry to God for self-control, yet ignore health guidelines. Perhaps we dismiss the Holy Spirit's prompting to glorify God in our flesh, to submit our body as a living sacrifice, holy and acceptable to God. Suppose we decide, though, to take God seriously, to glorify God in our body.

> God in the flesh is Christ in you, the hope of glory, in this present age in which we live.

Principle:
Jesus touches the believer through prayer, the Bible, other Christians, and the Holy Spirit.

Apply God's Word

1. Check the following physical challenges you face.
   ❑ Health
   ❑ Dietary habits
   ❑ Fleshly enslavements
   ❑ Exercise
   ❑ Other:

2. How seriously do you pray about the areas you checked above?

3. How familiar are you with what Christ teaches about the stewardship of your body?

4. To what degree do you take God's Word seriously that your body is Christ's temple and that you are not your own?

5. How open are you to health care professionals, pastors, teachers, friends, and family who express concern for your health or physical condition?
   ❑ I listen but don't pay much attention.
   ❑ I pay attention and prayerfully respond to concerns and advice.

6. What in particular needs to be modified in your body, mind, emotions, or will?

7. When the Holy Spirit nudges you to stop eating, what do you do?
   ❑ I stop.
   ❑ I continue.

8. When the Holy Spirit quickens your mind that you need to exercise, what do you do?
   ❑ Ignore Him.
   ❑ Get up and exercise.

9. When the Holy Spirit prompts you to order a healthy meal or stop drinking what is unhealthy, what do you do?
❏ What I want to do.
❏ What He prompts me to do, realizing that God, in compassion, is guiding me to better health.

As we consider Jesus' compassion toward Peter's mother-in-law, may we also consider His desire to exert a modifying influence on us as we face health issues and physical stresses.

Up Close and Personal
Thoughtfully record your answers to the questions below.

I may know intellectually that the Holy Spirit indwells me as a believer, but do I live in the instance of His presence, promptings, and help regarding my body, emotions, and lifestyle?

Am I taking the stewardship of my body as God's temple seriously, desiring to serve Him in my flesh?

Principle:
Jesus touched Peter's mother-in-law. He wants to touch us also . . . this instant.

A Prayer Opportunity
Will you let the cry of your heart go before God for Him to touch you this instant? Will you let the cry of your heart be that you want to dedicate your body and health in service to Him?

Day Four

Transformed

Mark 1:29–32

Father, as we continue to study Your Word today, may Your Word be life changing in us. Quicken our thoughts and spirits. Use Your Word to teach us. Transform us to be all that You raised us to be. Amen.

Thirty-eight-year-old Karla Faye Tucker, an ex-drug abuser and prostitute, was condemned to death for taking part in the pick-ax murders of Jerry Lynn Dean and Deborah Thornton of Houston in 1983. While in prison she received Christ as Savior, and the nation looked on as one woman was transformed by the power of God.

Not all transformations are outwardly as dramatic. However, the transformations might seem less different if we could see our sin as God does.

How does Christ transform a life? Do we have to wait for heaven to be transformed? Is there anything we can do to cooperate with the transformation process? **Read Mark 1:29–32.**

I love the different Gospel authors' wording of the same event. They each tell the same story, but inspired by the Holy Spirit, they notice different aspects of what Jesus did when He healed Peter's mother-in-law. Luke noticed how Jesus rebuked the fever. Matthew focused on how Jesus touched the suffering woman. What does Mark notice that is different from Luke and Matthew's accounts?

Mark notices that Jesus came to her. Jesus raised her up. Jesus took her hand. The fever left her. She waited on them.

What a beautiful portrayal of what Christ does in saving our souls and transforming our lives! A suffering woman was transformed into a serving saint! May the same be said of each of us!

As Mark recorded the transformation that came over Peter's mother-in-law, so other New Testament authors record the transformation process that comes over a person born of Christ.

First, Jesus came to Peter's mother–in-law, even as Jesus comes to us. The first observation is that Christ came to Peter's mother-in-law in her sickness. She could not get up

Disciples are not perfect men and women, but they do understand the call of God on their lives.

A suffering woman was transformed to a serving saint!

and go to Him, but He could go to her. In the same way, we cannot be transformed apart from Christ's coming to us and saving us.

Read Romans 5:8, then fill in the blanks with the words that show at what point Christ comes to us.

"God demonstrates His love toward us in that _____ we were _____ Christ died for us."

If we can capture the fact that our sinful nature is no surprise to God, it will tremendously help in our transformation process. As God loved us and Christ saved us while we were sinners, so God loves us and Christ saves us from our sinful habits. When we feel that we cannot go to God because we have sinned, the transformation process is slowed. Rather, we should run to God each time we fail. We should seek to learn from past failures. We should seek God's help in dealing with our sin and in standing against temptation.

Principle:
Jesus comes to us in the midst of our sin and weakness when we call on Him.

Second, Jesus raised Peter's mother-in-law. The process of transformation begins with Jesus coming to us and saving us. As Jesus raised Peter's mother-in-law, so Jesus raises us from death and eternity in hell to abundant and eternal life in Christ Jesus. **What is your favorite part of Ephesians 2:4–7?**

What do the following Scriptures say about a life transformed?

2 Corinthians 5:17

Colossians 3:9–10

Galatians 6:14–15

The Bible describes a Christian as transformed, a new creation, a new creature!

Principle:
Jesus raised Peter's mother-in-law to walk in newness of life. Jesus has raised the believer to walk as a new creation, in newness of life.

Third, Jesus took Peter's mother-in-law's hand. Jesus took Peter's mother-in-law's hand and transformed her. Her physical transformation was evidence of Christ's riches, grace, and kindness. Our lives should give evidence of Christ's hand on our lives, of the fact that Christ's Spirit is leading us.

The following Scriptures describe a person who is transformed by Christ as:

- A fragrance of Christ—2 Corinthians 2:15
- Having a life of liberty in the Spirit—2 Corinthians 3:17
- Not losing heart—2 Corinthians 4:1
- Having the light of God shining in their heart—2 Corinthians 4:6
- Having the power of God that is not of themselves—2 Corinthians 4:7
- Carrying about the life of Jesus in their body—2 Corinthians 4:10
- Manifesting the life of Jesus—2 Corinthians 4:10
- Focused on the eternal, not the temporal—2 Corinthians 4:18
- Putting to death the deeds of the body—Romans 8:13

Principle:
Jesus wants to take our hand and lead us to a transformed life.

Fourth, the fever left her. In Mark as well as in Luke 6:19 and other places, Christ's healing touch is identified with power.

How exciting it is to recognize Christ's transforming power is in the believer through the Holy Spirit!

Thoughtfully read the following Scriptures. Consider how Jesus' Spirit and power may be leading you to be transformed in some area. Check those that speak to your heart.

❏ **To be disciplined regarding the lusts of my flesh. Romans 13:14**
❏ **To be disciplined morally. 1 Corinthians 6:9-11**
❏ **To be disciplined regarding enslavements. 1 Corinthians 6:12**
❏ **To be disciplined in my body. 1 Corinthians 9:27**
❏ **To be disciplined when tempted. 1 Corinthians 10:13**
❏ **To be disciplined in regard to food and drink. 1 Corinthians 10:31**
❏ **To be disciplined in my thoughts. 2 Corinthians 10:5**
❏ **To be disciplined in my priorities. Philippians 3:7-8**
❏ **To be disciplined in my mind and emotions. Philippians 4:4, 6-9**
❏ **To be disciplined in my relationships. 1 Thessalonians 5:15**
❏ **To be disciplined in prayer. 1 Thessalonians 5:17**
❏ **To be disciplined spiritually. 1 Thessalonians 5:19**

When Jesus took Peter's mother-in-law's hand, the fever left her. When the Spirit of God leads us, plaguing sin leaves us.

Principle:
When the Spirit of God leads us, plaguing sin leaves us.

Fifth, she waited on them. Peter's mother-in-law was transformed from suffering in bed to serving the Lord. One of the main ways Satan defeats and discourages believers is through our body. As Satan tempted Jesus by offering Him the bread of disobedience, so we are tempted and fall through fleshly temptations Satan offers us.

Health problems are on the rise in our country due to the lack of discipline regarding what and how much we eat.

When we are ill we do not have the energy to serve the Lord as when we are healthy.

One of the many health problems our nation faces and that is often preventable is adult-onset diabetes. The implications of the increase of this disease are frightening, as the following excerpt from CNN.com, "One In Three Kids May Get Diabetes" reports.

Diabetes leads to a host of problems, including blindness, kidney failure, amputation and heart disease. Including undiagnosed cases, authorities believe about 17 million Americans have diabetes today. If the Center for Disease Control predictions are accurate, some 45 million to 50 million U.S. residents could have diabetes by 2050.

Dr. Kevin McKinney, director of the adult clinical endocrinological unit at the University of Texas Medical Center in Galveston stated, "There is no way the medical community could keep up with that. It doesn't have to happen. Type 2 diabetes can be prevented or delayed by losing weight, exercising and following a sensible diet."

If God's in control, why do so many people have diabetes and other diseases? Perhaps some people are born with a disposition toward certain ailments. Perhaps others indulge the flesh rather than exercise and eat whole foods God has given us.

As Satan tempted Jesus by offering him the bread of disobedience, so we are tempted to fall through the fleshly temptations he offers us.

Principle:
Jesus wants to bring our lives under His discipline so that we might know the blessing of serving Him and others.

Apply God's Word
The indwelling Christ, the Holy Spirit, is our hope for transformation. When a person comes to Christ, they find the Holy Spirit prompting physical changes in their life. No longer do they want to be at some of the same places they used to frequent. No longer do they want to be enslaved to fleshly habits.

Is your immediate response to being transformed by the power of God to serve Jesus? If not, why not?

Why is it important to be physically as well as spiritually changed? Through our bodies we serve Christ and walk in the works He has prepared for us to do.

In her sickened condition, Peter's mother-in-law could not serve Jesus. In her transformed condition, she immediately got up and served Jesus.

1. **Is your immediate response to being transformed by the power of God to serve Jesus? If not, why not?**

2. **How is Jesus reaching for your hand, to transform you physically, spiritually, or emotionally?**

3. **What plaguing sin needs to leave your life so you can serve Christ?**

Up Close and Personal
How might God's Word regarding the flesh be a compassionate warning to you?

How might God use you if and when you are at your best physically, spiritually, and emotionally?

Nutritionists recommend the very foods created for us by God. They are good foods, tasty foods. Yet society has become accustomed to fast foods, convenience foods, preservatives, fried foods, over-salted, and fat-saturated foods. Consider the following food selections that affect your health and, ultimately, your service to God. Circle the choice you most frequently make.

	Unhealthy Choice	Healthy Choice
Diabetes	Devil's Food cake	Delicious red apple
Heart Disease	Chicken fried steak	Baked chicken
Obesity	Almond Joy	Almonds
High Cholesterol	Fatty red meats	Fish, lean meats
Headaches	Diet soda	Water
Energy	Fast food	Fruit, whole foods

A Prayer Opportunity

May we each consider how Jesus wants to transform our lives to be physically as well as spiritually healthy. Speak to God about what is on your heart.

Day Five

Transformed to Serve Jesus

Mark 1:29–31, Luke 4:38–39, Matthew 8:14–17

Lord, the blessing of Your Word is that it challenges us. Thank You for the challenges it brings. Help us remember today that we belong to Christ. Help us remember our calling! Amen.

Today's study continues to highlight a woman known only as Peter's mother-in-law. Though unnamed to us, she is important in heaven. She knew our Lord. He visited her home. In compassion He touched and healed her of a suffering fever. In response, she served Jesus.

In studying the different accounts of Jesus healing Peter's mother-in-law, three Gospel authors have highlighted different aspects of her being healed. Matthew noted Jesus' touch. Mark noted Jesus' raising her up. Luke noted Jesus' rebuking her fever. Yet all three writers include one important point regarding what happened after she was healed. **What point do all three authors include? Mark 1:29–31, Luke 4:38–39, Matthew 8:14–17**

Today we are going to discover
- What it means to "wait on" or serve Jesus
- Triggers to our spiritual and physical health
- The ripple effect of serving Jesus

First, what does it mean to "wait on" or serve Jesus? The word *wait* in the New American Standard Bible and *minister* in the New International Version is the Greek word *dialoneo* and means "to serve" or "wait upon," with emphasis on the work to be done. Generally, it means "to do someone a service, care for someone's needs." One may work and not help anybody, but when *dialoneo* is used, helping someone directly is involved.

It is the same word used in Matthew 4:11 when the angels "ministered" or served Jesus after His forty days of fasting in the desert when the devil tempted Him. Can you imagine the joy of being able to serve Jesus and wait on Him at that time?

Serving Jesus is not only the privilege of angels. It was the privilege of Peter's mother-in-law. It is our privilege also. As believers we are able to serve the Son of God, as the angels did, as Peter's mother-in-law did!

Principle:
We can serve Jesus! We can care for His needs. We can serve others in a way that is advantageous to Jesus!

I do not know about you, but the privilege startles me. Jesus can use my help? It is beyond my understanding! How? Why? In what way? How does the thought that you can help Jesus, that you can directly serve Him, affect you? It makes me joyous! I want to run out the door, look up at the heavens and call out, "What can I do for You, Lord?"

Is it true that I can directly wait on Jesus as the angels did and as Peter's mother-in-law did? Join me as we look in the Bible and gain insight into our privilege of serving Jesus. If it is true that we can serve the Son of God, we are blessed beyond measure!

The following Bible passages use the same word, *dialoneo*, that is used in reference to the angels serving Jesus and Peter's mother-in-law serving Jesus. **Record what the Bible teaches** about serving. As you do, think in terms of your opportunity to serve Jesus!

Matthew 25:34–44 (*Dialoneo* is translated "care" in verse 44.)

Luke 8:3

Luke 17:7–10

Principle:
**In service, believers have the opportunity
to be a vessel through whom the Holy Spirit and
wisdom of Christ flow.**

The believer's desire and prayer should be for Jesus' Spirit and wisdom to flow from the wellspring of the indwelling Spirit to others. What promise did Jesus give in relation to the flow of His Spirit? **Write out your answer in first-person. John 7:38–39**

Jesus' intention is to live in us and have His Spirit flow through us! What intimacy! What a witness to the unbelieving world! God is love and wisdom. He communicates His love and wisdom through the Spirit-filled believer.

Principle:
**The believer can be a vehicle through whom Christ's
Spirit and wisdom flow upon others.**

Read Luke 4:38–41. After Jesus healed Peter's mother-in-law, what did she do?

Within what time period after she was healed did she serve Jesus?

What was the ripple effect of her serving Jesus?

Principle:
A ripple effect of service begins when a person Jesus has saved serves Jesus, which leads to others being saved and transformed by His Spirit and wisdom.

It is never too late and one is never too old to serve Jesus.

It is never too late and one is never too old to serve Jesus. I have precious memories of my 82-year-old mother, poised by the kitchen sink on her walker only a few days after being released from the hospital following congestive heart failure.

What was she doing? Washing rocks that were being prepared for our gift item, called The Cross Upon the Rock, to be shipped to New York. As she balanced against her walker and carefully washed each rock, God gave me a visual of a true servant. My mother wanted to be a part of what God was doing. She wanted to serve God's purposes in helping send rocks with the message of salvation across the country! Do we?

What a joy and privilege to hear Jesus' voice and commands, be touched by Him and transformed from suffering to serving in the fullness of Christ's Spirit and wisdom!

Apply God's Word
Why is it important for you, as a mother, daughter, friend, sister, wife, or coworker, to be full of the Spirit and wisdom?

In what ways do you model or not model the fullness of the Holy Spirit and wisdom?

Up Close and Personal

1. Do you listen to the promptings of the Holy Spirit regarding your body or do you rummage through the pantry and grab snack foods that lead to further cravings, irritability, and health decline? Underline positive triggers you need to develop.
- exercise
- drink plenty of water
- eat nutritious fruits, vegetables, nuts, whole grains, fish, and lean meats
- get needed sleep

2. What physical and spiritual choices can you make to create a more positive ripple effect for your service to Jesus?

3. Are you waiting to serve Jesus or serving Him now?

A Prayer Opportunity

Consider if you are serving Jesus as a response to His saving and serving you. Prayerfully speak to God if stress, food and drink, or not being filled with the Holy Spirit and wisdom contribute to any health problem or lack of spiritual vitality and service. Ask God to help you choose positive triggers for your body and spirit so that you might serve Jesus and others more fully in the Holy Spirit and wisdom.

Week Two
Thinking It Over

Please look back over your lesson and prayerfully complete the following.

1. What was most meaningful to you in your study of Peter's mother-in-law from:

Day 1

Day 2

Day 3

Day 4

Day 5

2. What most convicted or stirred your heart and mind this week?

3. Knowing that your health affects your ability to serve God, how is Jesus touching your heart to more responsibly manage:

what you eat and drink?

exercise?

4. Your lifestyle, amount of stress, response to stress, physical condition, even a headache, affects your service to God and others. How might Jesus want to transform you? In what way do you need to better respond to Jesus' guiding touch through the Holy Spirit, prayer, and His Word?

5. What "golden nugget" of truth do you want to remember?

6. What verse do you want to remember from this week's study?

7. What is the prayerful cry of your heart in relation to this week's study?

Week Three

When the Dark Clouds Roll In

Day One

Hannah

1 Samuel 1:1–2:21

How do we handle beautiful days being turned upside down? What do we do when it rains and pours and we are chilled by life and the darkness that envelops?

Father, thank You for the study of Your Word. Thank You for the examples of the women you give, who go before us and lead us in our faith. May we be ever so faithful to You as they were. May we know the blessing of intimacy with You as they did. In Jesus' name, Amen.

This summer as I stood on our back porch and watched the sun rise, I could not help but thank God for the beautiful, clear, crisp day. As I gazed at the clouds floating by, I felt a cool breeze; then I noticed more clouds gathering. Another cool breeze chilled my

arms. What a change from the hot days we had been having! I stood in awe and watched the clear sky transform to a dark and ominous power as a bolt of lightning flashed from heaven and rain pelted from the sky. In awe I praised God. In wonder I listened to the thunder as the dark clouds rolled in. My thoughts turned to a future day when the lightning will flash and the sky will roll back like a scroll to reveal the coming of our Lord.

On that day, those who have not acknowledged Christ as Lord will find their knees buckling. For those who have professed faith in Jesus as the Savior of the world, it will be a joyous reunion.

When the dark clouds roll in, where will you be in relation to God? Will you be ready? Will you be praising God? Will you know and understand it is the day of the Lord?

When the dark clouds roll in on our lives now, where are we in relation to God? Are we ready to accept the bad as well as the good? Are we praising or complaining? Do we know and realize that every day is the day of the Lord and we can trust our every day to Him, even when the dark clouds roll in?

The darkened sky was as much a wonder of God as was the blue sky. One woman understood that no matter what kind of weather was rolling in on her, the help she needed would not be found in anyone except God. Her name was Hannah.

In this week's study we will answer the following questions:

1. What triggers to despair can I guard against?
2. What steps can I take when I am in the midst of despair?
3. What can God bring from times of despair?

To begin, read 1 Samuel 1:1–2. It won't take you very long to get into this plot! For a background check on what we read, answer the following questions.

Tohu is the name of:
A. A food.
B. The great granddaddy of Elkanah.

Elkanah is the name of:
A. A man who had one too many wives.
B. Tohu's son.

Elkanah had:
A. Three fathers.
B. Two wives.

Peninnah is the name of:
A. A mountain range in Tohu.
B. Elkanah's wife who had children.

Now that we have the names of the people and places straight, let's begin! Ramah, where our story takes place, is located in the hill country of Ephraim, five miles north of Jerusalem.

Elkanah, one of the main characters in our account, is the husband of two wives. Their names were Hannah and Peninnah. Polygamy, the practice of taking multiple wives, was common in the ancient Middle East. Having many wives was a sign of wealth and rank. Often, multiple marriages were politically expedient for a king. Although polygamous marriages are recorded without direct comment throughout the Old Testament, they violate God's original intent for the marital relationship. Genesis 2:24 declares that a husband and wife should be one flesh. Jesus reiterated this principle in Matthew 19:5–6.

Although polygamy is incompatible with God's ideal, it apparently was allowed during Old Testament days in the case of a childless first marriage (Deuteronomy 21:15–17) and of a levirate marriage (Deuteronomy 25:5–10).

How many children did Hannah and Peninnah have?

Hannah:

Peninnah:

At this point in the story, one can imagine the potential problems this family has. What types of situations or emotional challenges might one face in these circumstances? **Continue reading in 1 Samuel 1:3.**

In this one verse we are given quite a bit of information! Elkanah went every year to Shiloh, 20 miles north of Jerusalem, which was the religious center of the nation until the loss of the ark (1 Samuel 4).

Why would Elkanah go to Shiloh? Find two reasons.
1)

2)

According to Exodus 23:14–18, three times a year male Israelites were required to appear at the central sanctuary for the festivals of Unleavened Bread, Pentecost, and Booths. However, during the period of the judges there appears to have been only one major pilgrim-festival (Judges 21:19). It is not stated which festival this was. **What type of sacrifice did God require?**

Exodus 23:18

Exodus 23:19

The sacrifice made to God was not to be made with leaven, a symbol of evil or sin. The sacrifice was to be made out of the choice first fruits. For Elkanah to "worship" meant that he not only took the expected sacrifice, but he bowed down. He prostrated himself before his superior, God, in homage. **How is God referred to in 1 Samuel 1:3?**

Charles Ryrie in the Ryrie Study Bible points out that "Lord of Hosts" is a military figure, referring to God as the One who commands the angelic armies of heaven and the armies of Israel. The term emphasizes the sovereignty and omnipotence of God.

At His outpost, His Tabernacle, the Lord of Hosts, the Lord of the angelic armies of heaven and the armies of Israel was to be worshipped. **Who were the two priests who would receive the sacrifices of Elkanah?**

Who was their father?

At this point it is important for us to understand the religious condition of the nation of Israel. **Read 1 Samuel 2:12, then** check the following that identifies what kind of priests Eli's sons were.

❏ Worthy
❏ Worthless

1 Samuel 2:12,13 explains why Hophni and Phinehas were worthless. **Fill in the blanks.**

They did not _____ the Lord and the _____ of the priests with the people.

What a sad statement! The priests, who were to have "worth," who were to ascribe "worth" to God by their lives, work, and worship by representing God to men and men to God, had no worth. They were "worthless," according to the Bible.

Why were they worthless? The Bible says they were worthless because they did not know God. What a powerful word of caution regarding what makes our life of value and worth!

The New Testament parallel to this passage is seen in the following verses. **Read John 17:3. What does Jesus say is of eternal worth? Fill in the blank.**

"This is eternal life, that they may _____You, the only true God, and Jesus Christ whom You have sent."

Just as it was important for the priests of the Old Testament to know God, so it is vital for us to know God, for in fact, knowing God and Jesus is eternal life. In addition, 1 Peter 2:9 explains that believers have a worthy responsibility in relation to Jesus and others. **Record 1 Peter 2:9, which describes the believer's role, in the first person.**

As a priest of God, a Christian is to be:
A. Worthless
B. Worthy, full of worth

What will make a Christian a worthy priest? 1 Samuel 2:12

Hophni and Phinehas did not know the Lord, though they served in the position of priests! Neither did they know the custom of the priests with the people. How sad! But how sad and true it can be in our day also, both of professional ministers and priests of God and Christians.

> **Principle:**
> Knowing God and God's ways
> should be the chief aim of each Christian.

Apply God's Word

As we look at the marriage and religious customs of the people and priests of Hannah's day, what marriage and religious parallels can you make to our day?

Marriage

Religious

Up Close and Personal

As we consider the priest's lack of knowledge of and obedience to God, we do well to consider how we are doing in our role as Christian priests of God.

1. How well do you, as a Christian, know God?

2. How worthily do you represent God's ways and customs to others?

A Prayer Opportunity

Pray and ask God to draw you close to His side as a demonstration of His ways, power, and discipline.

Day Two

When Depression Hits Home

1 Samuel 1:4–8

Lord, thank You for Your Word that opens our eyes and hearts, and directs our minds and steps. Show us the cleansing flow and powerful healing of Your Spirit and ways. Amen.

John Donne, an English clergyman and poet, stated, "No man is an island." Jesus warned that there would be tribulation in this world. Being a human being means facing challenging relationships, as well as challenging physical and emotional strains. The way we respond to the strains and tribulations of life defines our character.

Today, depression is an increasing concern to many. Depression is not only a concern for adults. It is an increasing health concern for teenagers and even children. The National Institute of Mental Health estimates there are nearly 2.3 million adolescents struggling with depression. Scientists say that early onset of depression in children and teens is increasingly common. Why? Some researchers think the stresses of a high divorce rate, rising academic expectations, and social pressures may push more kids over the edge. Depressed adolescents are at high risk for school failure, social isolation, promiscuity, "self-medication" with drugs or alcohol, and even suicide—the third leading cause of death among 15- to 24-year-olds.

What is the Christian community to do about this national

health issue? Anything?

The Bible clearly warns that there will be stress in the world, but God has provided for Christians in the midst of stress and tribulation. God has given us the Holy Spirit as a source of peace, power, and joy in the midst of stressful situations.

The Bible directs us what to meditate on in order to guard our hearts and minds. God has endowed each Christian with purposeful, meaningful work through their spiritual gifts. God has directed us to pray in response to stress and to not worry. The Bible tells us to be transformed, not conformed to the world, and tells us the key to transformation is a renewed mind.

But there is fire in the church. The fire is among the clergy and lay people. Depression is lit in the body. If believers do not control the fire it will continue to blaze and consume younger and younger people.

Triggers to depression are widespread. They can be biological or social. Sometimes the question is, "Which came first, the chemical imbalance or the emotional imbalance?" Regardless of which came first, in addition to spiritual help, there is help from the medical community for those living with depression.

For those who seek counseling, it is important to seek a well-trained Christian counselor. Treatment is available. But adhering to a healthy lifestyle prescribed by the Bible, counselors, therapists, and health care professionals can make a huge difference in the depressed person's life.

Christian women can make choices that will affect their emotional state:

- **Spiritually,** we can respond to the Holy Spirit, the Spirit of Christ abiding within us. We can respond to His promptings in regard to what we eat, drink, think, and do.
- **Mentally,** we can set our mind on the things above, where Christ is. We can think on those things that are true, honorable, right, pure, lovely, and of good repute, as the Bible directs us to do.
- **Emotionally,** we can follow the Bible's teaching and count it all joy when we encounter various trials, knowing that the testing of our faith produces endurance and endurance has its perfect result.
- **Physically,** we can eat whole foods God created to maintain

and stabilize our body, mind, and emotions—green vegetables, fresh fruits, water, lean meats and fishes, nuts, and grains. We can exercise and know the emotional benefit of natural feel-good hormones being released.

If we do those things that we know are right to do, does it mean we will never be sad? Does it mean we will never be overcome by grief or feel panicky? Does it mean we are always supposed to be happy? I think all of us would agree with Christ's words that in the world we have tribulation. In addition, the Bible teaches that our Heavenly Father disciplines those He loves. Discipline is not pleasant when it is being experienced, though the fruit of the disciplined life is.

Jesus wept. Peter wept. David wept. Hannah wept. And they were overcomers. Christian women have the opportunity to model the overcoming power of Christ in us, the hope of glory! May we learn from Hannah how to be an overcomer in the midst of suffering, provocation, and distress.

Read 1 Samuel 1:4-8. To refresh our memories, Elkanah's wife, Peninnah, has children. Hannah has none.

When Elkanah sacrificed, to whom did he give portions of the sacrifice?

What point of interest do you note about the portions that he gave?

We can picture the family scene! Elkanah, Peninnah, with *all* her sons and daughters, and then there is Hannah. Month after month, year after year, Hannah waited for the pregnancy that never came, while Peninnah bore children. Until you have waited, struggled, prayed, and sought medical attention for infertility, I do not believe there is any way to understand a woman's sorrow, frustration, disappointment, and hurt.

If not having children was not enough, Hannah faced additional sorrow and misery. **Use 1 Samuel 1:6 to answer the following questions.**

How is Peninnah described in the Bible?
A. As Hannah's friend
B. As Hannah's rival

Christians, as priests, are to be role models to the unbelieving world of the overcoming power of Christ in us, the hope of glory!

What did Peninnah do to Hannah?

Peninnah was not only insensitive; she was unkind and positioned herself as Hannah's rival. She "provoked" Hannah. One cannot help but feel extremely sorry for Hannah. **How does the Bible say Peninnah provoked Hannah?**
A. Unintentionally
B. Bitterly
C. Intentionally

Why did Peninnah provoke Hannah?
A. To tease her.
B. To irritate her.

Peninnah is far from being a kind woman! Unfortunately, there are people today like her, who intentionally hurt, irritate, and bring sorrow upon others. You may be living with one of those people. You may have a grown child who is one of those people. You may work with someone like Peninnah. Certainly, we do not want to be one of those people! If you think you are, if you intentionally hurt someone because you are jealous or angry, please use this time to carefully reflect and pray about who you are becoming. Ask God to give you grace to change. Take this moment to seriously alter your thinking and position in regard to whom you might be treating that way.

Peninnah had the blessing of children. Why then, might she have been so bitter? **Read 1 Samuel 1:4–5 to find two clues, then record your findings.**

Regarding Portions

Regarding Love

Peninnah had children, but not the love of her husband. Hannah had the love of her husband, but no children! Is that not the way life often is? We want perfect lives, spouses, children, homes, jobs, and finances. When life does not meet our expectations, we can become bitter, hard, and angry toward others and God. We can become depressed, alcoholics, overeaters,

short tempered. Or we can become better, sensitive to our high calling, to the Holy Spirit's controlling sway over us, released to God's will and daily provision.

In the account we are studying, we see two women in the same household and how they handle difficult situations in two very different ways!

During what time did Peninnah provoke Hannah?
A. When they were at home.
B. When they were going to the house of the Lord.

How many of us have experienced arguments on Sunday mornings before or on the way to church? Before we cast stones at Peninnah, we may need to examine our own hearts, our own tempers and temperaments. **Read 1 Samuel 1:7. How did Hannah respond to the provocation of Peninnah?**

Poor Hannah! There was nothing she could do—or was there? She could have argued with Peninnah. Hannah could have flaunted that she had the love of their husband. She could have taunted Peninnah. She could have used food as a source of comfort. She did not, though. What a woman of grace and a true priest of God!

Apply God's Word

1. What triggers to despair did Hannah have to guard against?

2. What responses did Hannah make in the midst of her despair?

3. What can you learn from observing both women?

Peninnah:

Hannah:

Up Close and Personal

1. Which woman are you—getting bitter or better?

2. What triggers to despair do you need to guard against?

3. What steps can you take when in the midst of despair?

A Prayer Opportunity

Prayerfully consider if you are ever like Peninnah. If you are, consider why. Take your reasons and triggers before God. Consider the Scriptures in light of your situation and role as a believer. Let the cry of your heart go before God. Ask Him to train your heart and mind how to respond in times of distress.

Day Three

When Food and Words Don't Comfort

1 Samuel 1:4–16

Lord, as we approach Your Word today, give us insight into the way we behave in relation to others and You. Amen.

"Eat something!" "It will be all right." "Snap out of it." Some of us have either said or heard those words from family or friends in an attempt to comfort or console us. However, are they words a person wants to hear when one is in the depths of sorrow or is being antagonized or provoked? Today, we will be reminded through Hannah's distressed state what to do when food and words do not comfort. We will be reminded of who is always present for us. We will be reminded that God can heal the wounded heart and set straight the mentally anguished.

Read 1 Samuel 1:3–8. As you recall, God designed going to the temple to be a time of celebration as the worshippers remembered God's faithfulness to past generations and His faithfulness to them. **However, what was on Elkanah, Peninnah, and Hannah's mind as they were enroute to Shiloh?**

Elkanah:

Peninnah:

Hannah:

Sometimes going to church can be a sorrowful time. A friend of mine shared with me how difficult it was for her to go to church and sit alone after her divorce. She shared how the pain was intensified as she watched other couples hold hands, sit with their children, and share the service together. Unfortunately, that can be the case. But in faithfulness to God, He also brings the reward of His presence. My friend was blessed as God led her to sit behind the deaf section. In doing so, she learned sign language and turned that training into signing God's praises, by which many have been blessed.

God does not require that we come to Him on a family plan, corporate plan, or even spouse plan.

Read 1 Samuel 1:8. What four questions did Elkanah ask Hannah in an attempt to comfort her?

Question # 1

Question # 2

Question # 3

Question # 4

Continue reading in 1 Samuel 1:9–10. Did Elkanah's words and gifts, though well intentioned, comfort Hannah? When the family arrived in Shiloh, Hannah had something to eat and drink. Her period of fasting was over, but not her grief. **How does the Scripture describe how she was feeling? 1 Samuel 1:10**

At this point in Hannah's life a great shift takes place. **Read 1 Samuel 1:9–18. Record Hannah's nine positive responses to**

the stress and distress she was experiencing.

Verse 9

Verse 10

Verse 11

Verse 12

Verse 13

Verse 15

Verse 16

Verse 18

These are all excellent responses to triggers of distress, depression, disappointment, provocation, and more! Let us look at each one more closely.

First, in her despair, Hannah took action. She went to God. Hannah went to God as the Source of her help for her deep sorrow and stress. She set her eyes on God rather than looking at and blaming others.

The body's physical reaction to stress, known as the "fight or flight" response, is helpful in the presence of imminent danger. However, chronic stress that we cannot fight nor flee, such as an unreasonable boss, a stormy relationship, or overwhelming responsibilities, can cause significant damage to the body. If the danger comes too often it can lead to damaged arteries, a weakened immune system, loss of bone mass, suppression of the reproductive system, and memory problems. May we follow Hannah's example and respond to problems with prayer, not stressful worrying.

Second, Hannah prayed to the Lord. As God's Word instructs us, we are to come to God in all circumstances and speak to the Lord our Maker, who is merciful and kind toward us. He is our compassionate Father and always has a listening ear.

Studies show that meditation, prayer, exercise, and relaxation techniques that take even a little pressure off the immune system can add up to a significantly healthier life. Christians can model the significantly healthier life of those who meditate on God and His counsel, who pray, exercise, and rest our minds and hearts in Him!

Third, Hannah wept bitterly. Studies have shown that those who are part of a rich social network have lower cortisol levels than loners, that people who pray regularly tend to live longer, and that breast cancer patients who have an optimistic attitude or an ability to express anger about their disease tend to live somewhat longer than those who do not.

Hannah poured out her hurt and bitterness. Her tension, disappointment, and grief had an outlet as she wept bitterly to the Lord. May we be mindful that we are not alone. May we practice expressing our anger, bitterness of soul, and despair to God who hears our prayers and sees our tears (2 Kings 20:5) and who takes account of those who pray and puts our tears in His bottle (Psalm 56:).

Fourth, Hannah sowed her tears with a vow of commitment. Hannah acknowledged her responsibility in relation to her prayer. Hannah asked for a son and committed to dedicate him to God.

It is important for believers to pray, but in addition to act in accordance with our prayers. If we pray for peace, do we also carefully choose our commitments? If we ask for our children to be "better," do we do our part to consistently instruct and discipline them in God's ways? If we ask for a stronger marriage, do we take time to be available to our spouse and not be constantly demanding? If we pray for a better job, do we work heartily as unto the Lord in our present job until He opens another door? If we pray to get out of debt, do we responsibly manage our money and not spend it on unnecessary purchases? If we pray for better health, do we responsibly eat, drink, and exercise?

Fifth, Hannah continued praying. I wish we were privy to

It is important for believers to pray, but in addition, to act in accordance with our prayers.

Persevering, heartfelt prayer is not only commended, it is taught.

what Hannah prayed as she continued her prayers to God. Did she ask for strength on the way home as she walked in the company of her family? Did she worship and praise God? We do not know what she prayed, but we do know that she continued praying. Repetitious, long prayers for the sake of show do not impress God. Persevering, heartfelt prayer is not only commended, it is taught, as we learn from 1 Thessalonians 5:17. Hannah teaches the power of being in the presence of God and the power of talking to God! Notice how she left her prayertime. Read 1 Samuel 1:18.

Sixth, Hannah spoke from her heart. There is nothing as powerful as deep, soul-wrenching prayers. Such prayers are not phony, "put on" words to our heavenly Father. They are honest, sincere words that flow from the depth of one's heart. To pour out one's soul is to bare all the honest thoughts going on in one's mind.

Is it not true that when talking with a counselor, friend, parent, child, or spouse, it often takes several minutes to get into a deep and meaningful conversation about what is on one's mind? Is it any wonder that for many people prayer is empty and stale because only a minute is given to prayer? Hannah spoke from her heart in continued prayer.

Seventh, Hannah poured out her soul and oppressed spirit to the Lord. To be oppressed is the Hebrew word, *qasheh,* and means to be unfortunate, melancholy, heavy, or sad in spirit. Many things can oppress us: sin, health, emotional struggles, over-commitments, financial burdens, children's struggles, tension in relationships, enslavements, and on and on. Rather than keeping her despair bottled up, which can lead to physical problems, Hannah poured out her soul to the One who lifts her head!

When you are down, do you blow up or look up, get drunk or pray, eat unhealthily or feed on the counsel of God? May we learn from the saints who expressed their anger and hurts, and who called out to God in their hopeless situations and were heard.

Eighth, she prayed out of great concern and provocation. Hannah acknowledged the Lord of Hosts, faithful in the past, to be faithful to her in her present oppression and barrenness. Her prayer indicated her faith as she dedicated the first fruit of her womb as a priest unto God, a son of a Levite, a Nazarite.

Hannah was concerned about the stressful triggers in her family, the provocations, bad relationships, and her barrenness. She did not cover up or ignore the problems She did not use mind over matter, suppress what was going on, and repeat as a mantra, "I am happy and fine." Rather, Hannah came to God at the altar of prayer and met Him in sincerity and truth.

Ninth, she went her way and ate, and her face was no longer sad. Hannah did not carry her burdens home. She left her burdens in God's hands. Hannah is a model of giving one's worries to God and trusting Him with the outcome! When Hannah left the temple, not one single circumstance in her life was different, but she was. She walked into the temple with a stressful family, a stressful marriage, and barrenness. She walked out of the temple with a stressful family, a stressful marriage, and barrenness. Why the change in her countenance? Why was her face no longer sad? Why was she able to go her way, eat, and return to her same situation no longer sad?

In Geoffrey Cowley's article, "The Science of Happiness," (*Newsweek*, September 16, 2002) he states that our moods revolve around the emotional baselines or "set points" we are born with, and that our circumstances in life have little to do with the satisfaction we experience. However, later he notes that married churchgoers tend to outscore single nonbelievers in happiness surveys. Could it be that those who are born of the Spirit are able to live beyond the norm "set range"? Can our countenance be changed as Hannah's was through prayer? Our children, family, and friends are watching! May our faces reflect our faith!

> When Hannah left the temple, not one single circumstance in her life was different, but she was.

Apply God's Word

What has been your experience when greatly distressed, like Hannah? Have others ever tried to comfort you with words or food? How effective were they at relieving your distress or grief?

Consider Hannah's nine responses to distress. Which of her responses prompted the greatest thought in you? Which

response do you need to act on?

Up Close and Personal

1. What priority do you place on sincerely pouring out your soul to the Lord as you look at His past faithfulness, and anticipate His faithfulness to you in the future?

I have found that highlighting God's answers to prayers in my prayer journal is a tremendous faith builder and help in times of hope and despair.

2. What response to distress, grief, or provocation does God desire you make in order for you to become better, not bitter or depressed?

3. What responsible action in accordance with your prayer is in order?

Journaling your commitment in relation to your prayer helps one stay focused and responsible before God. For instance, when you record "Lord, help me eat right, be self-controlled, look to You, be better, not bitter," it serves as a reminder of how God has spoken to your heart and mind. As you journal, you can check yourself against what God has prompted you to pray and do. By listening to the counsel and comfort of God, we can be changed! We learn to abide in Christ as we learn to discern the prompting of the Holy Spirit in us.

A Prayer Opportunity

Take this time to pour out your heart to God about any burden or stresses you have. Listen to God's counsel for you. Record your responsibility to God in accordance with your prayer.

Day Four

A Woman of Honor and Excellence

1 Samuel 1:12–20

Father, as we seek Your presence and Word today, reveal Your love and ways, that we may walk in them. Amen.

Feelings of despair can lead us to make unhealthy choices. In times of stress, marital difficulties, childrearing problems, boredom, loneliness, or financial pressures we can turn to food, alcohol, excessive work or exercise, television, lethargy, or excessive activities to help us forget, numb our pain, elevate our mood, and help us deal with life. Many of those, if not all, can be harmful when abused or carried to extremes. No substitute can take the place of our body, mind, and soul being at peace, filled with God's Spirit of love, hope, faith, and joy.

In today's study we are going to be challenged by Hannah's honor and excellence. May we strive to live before the Lord in the way she did! **Reread 1 Samuel 1:12–16 to refresh your memory of the text, then answer the following questions.**

What did Eli assume when he saw Hannah praying?

Why might Eli have assumed Hannah was drunk, just by watching her?

What did Eli tell her to put away, assuming she was drunk?
A. Her Kleenex
B. Her wine

How much had Hannah had to drink?
A. None
B. A jug

Hannah had not poured herself wine or strong drink. What had she poured?

Hannah was concerned when Eli thought she was drunk. Which of the following ways was she concerned he might think of her?
A. As a worthless woman
B. As a temple prostitute

The word *worthless* in the NASB is *wicked* in the NIV and *Belial* in the KJV. It is interesting to note that in the KJV, 1 Samuel 1:16 reads, "Count not thine handmaid for a daughter of Belial…" Hannah did not want Eli to "count" her as worthless or wicked. On the other hand, 1 Samuel 2:12 states, "Now the sons of Eli were sons of Belial…" Eli's sons were wicked and worthless!

Hannah was not worthless! She knew the Lord! Her life counted for Him, even though she had no children, lived in a difficult family, and had worthless priests. Her self-esteem was not tied up in the temporary world, but in the eternal God! Is yours?

Principle:
The Christian's worth is not tied to things or persons, but to the Lord.

Hannah, who poured out her soul in the Tabernacle, was more of a priest and of more value than were the temple priests, Hophni and Phinehas. Hannah pointed people to God. Hannah, pouring out her soul to God rather than giving in to drink or despair, prayed and received back what was of value to God.

The more you and I make healthy spiritual, physical, and emotional choices in the midst of despair in our homes, churches, and society, the more valuable we are in pointing others to God. The more we serve as God's priests, representing men to God and God to men, the more worthwhile our lives are in God's kingdom! What an honor and privilege we have before us! May we live worthy lives, pointing others to God in the midst of despair.

After Hannah explained to Eli that she was not drunk, he responded differently to her. **What did Eli say to Hannah?**

A remarkable change takes place in Hannah in 1 Samuel 1:18. **Check the true statements.**

❏ She refused to speak further with Eli, who heaped insult upon her hurt, and who had no right to accuse her of drunkenness since his own sons were worthless.

❏ She vowed never to go to the Tabernacle again and worship with such hypocrites.

❏ She respectfully responded to Eli, seeking favor in his sight.

❏ She went her way.

❏ She ate.

❏ She drank a jug of wine.

❏ Her face was drawn and sad from the emotionally exhausting day!

❏ Her face was no longer sad.

❏ She arose early the next morning and worshiped before the Lord.

❏ She returned to her house in Ramah.

❏ She gave up trying to bear a child and harbored resentment toward Elkanah.

❏ She and Elkanah "had relations."

The choices we make reflect our faith. We are to pray, but then we are to act in accordance with our prayers. Do you pray for discipline, but then refuse to suffer even an hour of deprivation? Do you pray for joy, but continue to replay past wrongdoings in your mind? Do you ask God to remove the guilt of your sin, but then visit your wrongs like tombstones at a cemetery, grieving over them? Do you have stress-induced illnesses and have yet to get on your face and pour your heart out to God and ask Him how to meet those stresses? Do you pray your children will make better decisions in regard to food and drink, but do not model what you pray for them?

The choices we make reflect our faith.

> **Principle:**
> We are to pray,
> then act in accordance with our prayers.

Hannah prayed. Then she responded in faith according to her prayers. **Read 1 Samuel 1:19. Who remembered Hannah?**
A. Hophni
B. Phinehas
C. The Lord

We can count on the Lord to remember us! At times we may feel forgotten, but our Lord never forgets us. We are on God's mind and heart. **As a matter of fact, what does Jesus do for us? Hebrews 7:25**

We are on God's mind and heart.

Does God sleep? Will God not keep you? Will God not guard you? **Read Psalm 121:1–8** to be blessed by the beautiful reminder of where our help comes from and of God's remembering and keeping us! **Record Psalm 121:1–2,** wonderful verses to memorize!

The faithfulness of God is seen when He remembers Hannah. In the perfect time, His time, at the perfect point in history, God's point, He answered Hannah's prayer. The question is sometimes asked, "Did God cause Hannah's infertility?" The Quest Study Bible answers that question with the following explanation. "The view that God had closed her womb may have stemmed from a Hebrew view of life that saw God as the primary cause behind everything—even if the outcome was tragic or evil. Today we might say God permitted but did not cause Hannah's infertility. Though God may not answer every childless couple as he did Hannah and Elkanah, he always has their best interest at heart."

Hannah bearing a son in God's timing is one of numerous examples in the Bible of God's sovereignty. May we trust God as we go through the days of our lives. May we acknowledge Him as Sovereign Lord who has the right and power to act in accordance with His kingdom and purposes. **Read 1 Samuel**

1:20. What happened in "due time"?

What did Hannah name their son?

Why did she name him that?

The name Samuel means "name of God" and served as a continual reminder of God's mercy toward those who call on His name. May we each know the blessing Hannah did as we call on God's name in the midst of despair, depression, or oppressive times of life!

Apply God's Word

Contrast Hannah, Eli's sons, and yourself in the chart below.

	Hannah	Hophni and Phinehas	Yourself
Sincerity in sacrifice and worship			
Lifestyle and habits in the midst of stress, boredom, depression			
Worth/worth-lessness in pointing others to God			

If you fall short of Hannah's example, what positive steps could you take to make your life more worthwhile in God's kingdom and to better point family, friends, coworkers to God?

Physically:

Emotionally:

Spiritually:

Up Close and Personal
Our lives are in view of our friends, coworkers, family, pastors, and even strangers. Do your actions and choices point others to worship God sincerely even in the midst of stress and despair? What do others see in you?

Do you pray, then act in accordance with your prayers? In what way do you need to act more responsibly in accordance with your prayers?

A Prayer Opportunity
Pour out your heart in sincerity and truth before the Lord. Prayerfully consider how God is calling you to act in accordance with the prayer of your heart.

Day Five
The Outcome of Faith
1 Samuel 1:21–2:11

Lord, You have taught us that we can know You, the God of all comfort. You have taught us that we can pour out our heart and tears to You. Thank You for the outcome You bring in the midst of despair. Amen.

Just when you think a story could not get better, it does! The account of Hannah is one such story. God took her from a state of depression, provocation, and being misunderstood to a place of joy, peace, and exultation. What was the connecting

source? Was the connecting source her husband or the priests?

The Lord of Hosts was the connecting link between Hannah's desperation and her joy! Hannah responded to the stressful triggers of her life by turning to God and acting in accordance with her prayer. God honored Hannah.

As we recall, Hannah had a number of stressful triggers that could have plunged her into depression and poor choices. We are aware of two of them: living with someone who bitterly provoked her, and being infertile. When we consider the series of right choices she made in the midst of her circumstances, we are amazed. We can also be encouraged that we can make the right choices in the midst of our circumstances. If and when we fail, we can turn and make the right choice the next time!

There is nothing recorded about Peninnah, the provoking, contentious wife and her children after 1 Samuel 1:7. What was the fruit of her bitterness? Nothing.

What was the fruit of Hannah's life? Samuel, who grew to serve the Lord of Hosts, who called the people to a revival of the true worship of the Lord, who anointed Saul as the first king of Israel and who anointed David, king of Israel.

What was the outcome of Hannah's life, of her trusting God in the midst of daily provocation and despair? The outcome of Hannah's faith is expressed in the writings of Paul. **Read Romans 5:1–5 and record blessings that are the outcome of faith.**

Verse 1

Verse 2

Verse 3

Verse 4

Verse 5

The outcome of Hannah's life was:
• Faith and peace with God
• Learning to exult in hope
• Learning to exult in tribulation
• Perseverance

• Proven character
• Hope
• The love of God being poured out within her through the Holy Spirit

What can we learn from Hannah? We can learn how important it is to our mental, spiritual, emotional, and physical health to respond to triggers of depression, stress, and temptation in the way God teaches us. We can learn that we can be blessed, as Hannah was, even through times of despair. We can learn that the outcome of our faith can be that we know God better, He who can bring about good even through the worst of times.

We learn that our faith is supposed to mean something. Faith is not a certificate we receive when we join a church. Although the ultimate outcome of our faith is the salvation of our souls, there is to be a daily outcome of our faith, also. Faith, in its truest sense, produces something. God can use the stresses of the world to bring forth the witness of His Son and Spirit in us! When we are stressed or depressed, we have the opportunity to practice walking in God's ways. The result is joy and peace in the Holy Spirit.

> **Perhaps the reason we fall short in our Christian walk is because we do not expect outcomes of our faith.**

Principle:
Our faith is to have an outcome!

The outcome of Hannah's faith was not only a son. An even greater outcome of her faith was learning that the Lord is full of compassion and is merciful. May we each learn who the Lord is through the testing of our faith, the temptations of the world, and the provocations of our spirit and soul!

Hannah learned of God's compassion and mercy through her prayers. **Read 1 Samuel 1:20. To what did Hannah attribute giving birth to Samuel?**

Consider how special each day and year must have been to Hannah as she washed Samuel's little toes, sang to him, and held him to her breast. Consider how she must have gently

talked to Samuel about the Lord of Hosts and Samuel's calling as she pointed out the birds and trees and taught him that all things were created by God and for God. Are we doing that with our children? Do we even understand that about our own life?

Think about what Hannah must have said when Samuel scraped his knee and cried, of how she must have drawn him into her arms and taught him that God hears our cries. Consider how Hannah taught Samuel to respond to negative remarks and criticism. Think about how she taught Samuel not to seek the approval of those who are bitter, but rather to live out the fullness of godliness in their presence better. Are we modeling to be better, not bitter?

Consider how Hannah taught Samuel to pray about anything, to pour out his little heart to the Lord when frustrations mount, feelings are hurt, and depression looms. Do we teach that to our children and others by the witness of our life?

What good is our faith? Is our faith for one hour of church or is it for hearing the voice of the Lord and Him guiding our steps and filling our hearts through good and bad days? What are we teaching our children and those who are not Christians?

Are we modeling being over-committed, placing undue stress on ourselves, and then responding in emotional outbursts or abuse of food or drink or sickness or depression? What are we teaching by the demonstration of our life? Are we teaching by example to eat healthy, to exercise our bodies and minds, to use God's Word as the foundation of decisions, and to live for Christ?

As we ponder these and more questions in light of Hannah's life, we must ask ourselves, "What is the outcome of our faith?" The words of 1 Samuel 1:24–28 give further insight into the outcome of Hannah's faith. Does Hannah sound like a bitter woman with sour grapes who resents her vow to the Lord? No.

Samuel was young but his life had been dedicated to the Lord. Samuel no longer depended on his mother's milk to live. He would now learn to depend on God for his life. We can only imagine the provision God made for his tiny heart the first night he laid his head down to sleep. How the angels must have hushed him to sleep. How the God of all comforts must have cradled his spirit in peace.

The outcome of our faith is proved when we trust God through the difficult times, not when things are going our way.

Perhaps the reason we fall short in our Christian walk is because we do not expect outcomes of our faith. We do not expect God to be faithful. When we do have faith, we demand immediate results. Perhaps we can learn from Hannah that the outcome of our faith is not always immediate. The outcome is often hard, but our Heavenly Father is faithful!

What was the outcome of Hannah's faith as she turned loose of the tiny hand of Samuel and turned him over to the Lord of Hosts? Join me as we take a peek inside her heart.

Slowly read 1 Samuel 2:1–10, Hannah's song. As you do, put yourself in her place. Listen carefully to the song in her heart, to the knowledge she has of God in her soul. Would you have been rejoicing or bemoaning your vow? The outcome of Hannah's faith is that she exalts the Lord! **Read 1 Samuel 2:1–10, then answer the following questions.**

Verse 1: In whom and what does her heart exalt and rejoice? How often do you remember to rejoice in God and your salvation when there is nothing else to rejoice in?

Verse 2: Who does Hannah compare to the Lord? Who is the rock, the sure, strong foundation of her life? On what or whom do you depend?

Verse 3: Who does Hannah know God to be and why? What consolation is that to you?

Verse 4–9: In praise, what power does Hannah attribute to the Lord? What do her words, "Not by might shall a man prevail," mean to you?

Verse 10: How would you summarize Hannah's praise and exaltation of the Lord?

The outcome of Hannah's faith through times of distress was being intimately acquainted with the Lord of Hosts! The final outcome of Hannah's faith is seen in 1 Samuel 2:11–12. In the

midst of worldly pressures and corrupt priests, Hannah raised a child who served the Lord!

Every year Hannah took Samuel a little robe that she made for him. **Read 1 Samuel 2:26. Record the blessed words of the verse.**

Who else are these words spoken about? Luke 2:52

Are they words spoken about us?

Principle:
The outcome of our faith is to produce growth in stature and favor with God and men.

The world is our schoolhouse. The Lord is our teacher. The Bible is our textbook. The Holy Spirit is our helper, mentor, and prompter. May we face the trials and provocations of our spirit in a way that will model to those who are watching the testimony of Hannah. May we model prayer, not self-pity, becoming better, not bitter. May we model dropping to our knees, not dropping out of life. May we model hope, not hopelessness!

Apply God's Word
The outcome of our faith is proved when we trust God through the difficult times, when things are not going our way. Check the times it would have been easy for Hannah to choose the wrong response to stressful triggers. Under the ones you check, record what Hannah could have done if she had responded in her flesh. In the second blank, record how you might have responded.

When she was bitterly provoked by Peninnah, Hannah could have:

I might have:

When Hannah arrived at Shiloh, instead of going to the temple to pray,
Hannah could have:

I might have:

In her oppressed spirit, instead of continuing in prayer until she was consoled, another source of consolation could have been sought.
Hannah could have:

I might have:

After she left the temple, instead of leaving with a changed countenance,
Hannah could have:

I might have:

When Hannah and Elkanah returned to Ramah, rather than trying to get pregnant,
Hannah could have:

I might have:

After giving birth to Samuel, rather than weaning him and dedicating him to the Lord,
Hannah could have:

I might have:

After dedicating Samuel to the Lord, rather than raising her voice in worship and praise,
Hannah could have:

I might have:

Up Close and Personal

In what way does Hannah's life challenge you?

What outcome might the Lord want to produce in you in the midst of your struggles or distress or provocation?

A Prayer Opportunity

Pray about what the Lord has most impressed on your mind through today's study, focusing on the outcome of your faith He seeks.

Week Three
Thinking It Over

Please look back over your lesson and prayerfully complete the following.

1. What was most meaningful to you in your study of Hannah from:

Day 1

Day 2

Day 3

Day 4

Day 5

2. How did God convict, stir, or prompt your heart and mind by Hannah's life?

3. What triggers to despair or discouragement do you need to guard against?

4. What outcome of your faith might God be trying to bring forth in the midst of your physical, emotional, financial, or other distress?

5. What "golden nugget" of truth do you want to remember from this week?

6. What verse do you want to remember from this week's lesson?

7. What is the prayerful cry of your heart in relation to this week's study?

Week Four

When Nothing Seems to Help

Day One

The Woman with the Issue of Blood

Matthew 9:20–22, Mark 5:21–34, Luke 8:43–48

When nothing works, not medication, doctor's advice, nor friend's home remedies, what do you do? What can you do?

Father, when we are desperate we seek You. Teach us to have faith and seek You not only when we are hurting or sick, but to seek You all the time. May we come to You in faith, expecting You to work all things together for good as we love You. Amen.

One chilly, rainy morning when the black clouds rolled in, I decided to brew a cup of green tea. Having never tried green tea, I read the label with interest. "100 percent natural! Orange, passion fruit and jasmine." The label made it sound as yummy

as a Caribbean island drink! As I continued reading, my mind wandered to prior days of coffee and chocolate-glazed doughnuts. Yum yum! I had not longed for a doughnut in quite some time, but the weather thrust me into my old desires and tastes! Green Tea . . . the new me!

As I reined my wandering mind from doughnuts to the little green box in hand, I continued to discover more about my newfound friend . . . green tea!

"Green is good," a cute little leaf told me. "Green is clean," another chimed in. "This is great," I thought to myself. "I need good and clean!" I read on. Perhaps the encouragement would inspire me to gulp several cups.

"Green tea contains natural flavonoid antioxidants." "What," I wondered, "is a flavonoid? Antioxidants . . . hmm," I mused to myself. As I continued reading I began to feel the tea was less like a Caribbean drink and more like medication! The little leaf continued, "The tea contains flavonoid antioxidants to help neutralize free radicals." At the thought of free radicals, I immediately conjured in my mind a group of radical people waving their signs in the air and chanting.

"Hmm, this little green tea is going to do all this for me?" I wondered as I continued to fight thoughts of coffee and doughnuts. Back to my free radical flavonoid, antioxidant drink. (And all I had wanted to do was curl up with a nice comfy drink before I began my day.)

The leaf continued to explain that it would fight molecules that could damage my healthy cells. I brewed and I stewed my little cup of tea, then sat down for a first sip. "Hmm." Well, what can you expect from a little cup of green tea?

God expects us to take care of our bodies. God has a right to expect us, as stewards of our bodies, to make good nutritional choices. But even when we do, that does not guarantee that in the process of aging, accidents, and this world we will avoid pain and disease.

The woman with the issue of blood, whom we are studying this week, had lived with her condition for years. She is seeking help when we meet her in Mark 5:25–34. **Read Mark 5:25–34** to learn about the woman with the issue of blood.

This is one of the sweetest accounts in the Bible. We can imagine the desperation of her soul prior to going to Jesus. We can smile, rejoicing with her as Jesus blessed her with the words, "You are healed!"

God has a right to expect us, as stewards of our bodies, to make good nutritional choices.

In this week's study we are going to consider the answer to the following question: When nothing works, not healthy foods, medications, or treatment, what can we do? **To fully appreciate our text, read the background passage, Mark 5:21–24.**

At this time Jesus was not preaching in the synagogue. Rather, where was He? Mark 5:21

Jesus had been teaching on the southeast side of the Sea of Galilee where He had healed a demon-possessed man. Then He crossed over to the west side where we find Him in Mark 5:21. Galilee is the name of both an area of land and a large lake in northern Israel. It was the home area of Jesus and a number of His disciples. When His public work began, Jesus spent much of His time there. It was surrounded on three sides by other nations and strongly influenced by them. Most of Galilee is hilly, but the land falls steeply to 600 feet below sea level around the lake.

In Jesus' time, several major roads of the Roman Empire crossed Galilee. Farming, trade, and the lakeside fisheries were the main industries. Many of the towns and villages mentioned in the Gospels are in Galilee, including Nazareth (where Jesus grew up), Capernaum, Cana, and Bethsaida. The lake, which is susceptible to sudden fierce storms as the wind funnels through the hills, is the place of our study today.

In 1998 my family had the privilege of traveling to Israel and taking a boat across the Sea of Galilee. You can imagine the awe we felt as we walked where Jesus walked and went in a boat across the lake Jesus walked upon.

To look back at the times, places, and events in Jesus' life through the Bible is inspiring. To stand on the shore where Jesus cast out demons and healed a desperate woman who sought Him is most moving!

I invite you back to Israel with me. I invite you to travel back in time 2000 years. Travel past the day of the space shuttle, airplane, and car. Travel to the day of the camel, when people walked miles to hear a prophet of God. Travel back, far from the day of sophisticated hospitals and medications. Travel to a dusty road, hilly land, and a time and place in which women were not highly regarded and religious status meant everything. Travel back to a time of pain in your life.

Travel in your pain outdoors, following the crowd, pleading in your heart and praying in your mind to get a glimpse of Jesus.

Then, just when you think you may see Jesus, who walks briskly past you? **Read Mark 5:22.** A synagogue official has taken your place and the hope you had to see Jesus. He is earnestly seeking Jesus just as you are. You observe Jairus with Jesus. **What does he do? Mark 5:22**

In earnestness and humbleness, Jairus has come to Jesus with a plea. **What is his need and request of Jesus? Mark 5:23**

Your hope to see Jesus wanes. Certainly Jairus, an important synagogue official, has priority over you, a common unclean woman. Without doubt, Jairus' need is more important than your issue of blood. Downcast, you consider turning and going home, but then, reconsider. You press forward in the crowd, following Jesus. Perhaps if you could just touch Him!

Principle:
Every person has a chance to follow Jesus.

Apply God's Word

How would you describe who Jesus is to you? Is He a historic religious figure, a symbol of goodness, one of many equally wise prophets of old?

How would you describe your relationship to Jesus? Do you reverence Him? Do you follow Him in your need? Do you look for where Jesus is working in people's lives and seek Him out, as the woman did?

Up Close and Personal

1. Who in reality is Jesus to you on a day-to-day basis?

2. Would you have persevered and sought Jesus had you been the woman with the issue of blood?

3. In what ways are you presently seeking Jesus? Are you too occupied with other things?

A Prayer Opportunity

Consider if you would have stayed home the day Jesus came to your area. Today, we do not have to travel or push through crowds to be in Christ's presence. Prayerfully take advantage of this moment to be in Christ's presence, and tell Him your thoughts and needs.

Day Two

In the Midst of Suffering
Mark 5:24–28

Father, we bow with Your Word before us and seek Your face. Teach us the reality of Your concern for each person. Revolutionize our attitude regarding suffering, weakness, and the dark times of our life! May we be vessels of Your glory and power in the dark times of our life. Amen.

When nothing works, not healthy foods and drinks, medications, or treatment, what can we do? Is God in control? Is there any help?

As tots at Barbara Ann's Dance Studio, one of the first things ballerinas learned was first, second, third, and fourth positions. Those positions were basic to future dance steps. In our tutus, we pointed toes and developed balance, and increased our coordination and poise. I am glad for the lessons

I learned at Barbara Ann's. They introduced me to physical grace.

As a little one in Sunday school I learned the basics about Jesus. I learned the four spiritual laws. I was a sinner. I could not get to heaven on my own. Jesus loved me and gave His life for me on the cross. I could be saved. Those truths were the foundation for future spiritual growth. I am glad for the lessons I learned as a child at church. They introduced me to spiritual grace.

The harder lessons at Barbara Ann's and church came later. At Barbara Ann's it was how to dance on my toes. With God, it was how to walk in the darkness. I am glad for the lessons at Barbara Ann's. I learned I could dance on my toes, with the right toe shoes on. I am glad for my lessons with God. I learned I could walk in the darkness, with the Father holding my hand.

Today, we will focus on an advanced spiritual teaching. We will learn that the dark, trying times of our life provide an opportunity for God to be glorified. Today, Christians in America do not fight gladiators in the coliseums of Rome because of our faith. We are not sawn in two nor fed to lions. We are not tortured to see if we will recant our faith.

How then, do we demonstrate our faith? What does the world see when we are prodded and poked, stuck and maimed, sick and dying, or living in sufferable conditions as the woman in our study is?

I joyfully report to you that the medical community now recognizes that Christians are unique! Researchers at Georgetown University School of Medicine found that at least 80 percent of the studies they did suggested spiritual or religious beliefs have a beneficial effect on health. The researchers concluded that people who consider themselves spiritual:
- Enjoy better health
- Live longer
- Recover from illness more quickly and with fewer complications
- Suffer less depression and chemical addiction
- Have lower blood pressure
- Cope better with serious disease, such as cardiovascular disease.

How exciting for Christians to be proven different, above the norm! But how could these statistics be proved if Christians did not suffer the same tribulation as unbelievers?

> ## Principle:
> **Suffering provides an opportunity
> for the glory of God to be proved.**

Read Mark 5:24–28. What was the woman's physical condition? Mark 5:25

The unnamed woman in our account suffered. Literally, she "was in" bleeding for 12 years. This may have been a chronic menstrual disorder called menorrhagia, the scientific word for excessive uterine bleeding. It could have been accompanied by endometriosis, a common and often painful disorder of the female reproductive system. Left undiagnosed or untreated, painful periods can cause a woman to miss work or school and can strain relationships. Recurring pain can lead to depression, irritability, anxiety, anger, and feelings of helplessness. Infertility linked to endometriosis can cause emotional distress.

Twelve years! Can you imagine? Some of you who have suffered a chronic illness or pain for twelve years or more can empathize with this dear woman. For those who have not, think for a moment what it would be like in her day to suffer in such a way. One might wonder if there were no doctors available for her to go to. **Was that the case? Mark 5:26**
❏ Yes
❏ No

The Scripture tells us that there were doctors and, as a matter of fact, she had been to many of them! **What kind of treatment had she found effective over the past twelve years? Mark 5:26**

Although the woman had been to many doctors, she had not been helped. **What does the Scripture say about her experience with the doctors? Mark 5:26**
❏ She found help.
❏ She endured much at the hands of many physicians.
❏ She had grown worse.

The physician, Luke, in his account of this woman in Luke 8:43 states very clearly that she could not be cured by anyone. She lived with an incurable disease and with no hope of a cure. **Imagine how this woman felt! Record your thoughts.**

Going to the doctor with any problem is stressful. Why would it have been especially humiliating and grueling for a woman in her day to live month after month, year after year, hemorrhaging? **See Leviticus 15:25–28 for help with your answer.**

The hemorrhaging woman's condition made her ritually unclean, meaning that she was excluded from normal social relations since any who came in contact with her would become ceremonially "unclean." **Consider how you would feel physically, spiritually, and emotionally if you were her. Physically:**

Spiritually:

Emotionally:

It makes us want to cry for her. More than likely she shed many tears on her bed at night and through the day in her suffering. For those of you who have taken care of a hemorrhaging condition, you know the constant attention and cleansing required. The care can be exhausting, let alone the fatigue and anemia associated with twelve years of hemorrhaging.

In addition, imagine being a socially "unclean" person. To feel unclean all the time, to be isolated or ignored, perhaps looked down upon, would have added insult to injury.

Possibly the worst hurt, however, would be to wonder why, to ask God what you had done to deserve such suffering. When I was twenty-nine and diagnosed with ovarian cancer, the first question that raced through my mind was "Why?" My thoughts turned to every unhealthy habit and sin I had ever committed. Guilt grew in me until God flooded me with His peace and love.

Did this woman recount her sins? Did she beg forgiveness for acts of sin as well as those she only imagined were sin?

Did she wonder why God did not heal her? Did she wonder why she suffered and others did not? Did she look out the window and wish she could go to the synagogue, wish she could have normal relations; wish just one doctor could help her? Nowhere does the Scripture say that this woman's condition was caused by her sin.

Perhaps you are suffering. What comfort can the Bible give you about suffering? What can your outlook be in the midst of suffering that will give glory to God?

Read Romans 8:18–39, a passage on expectant living. Record thoughts from the passage that encourage you and direct your thoughts to the hope that is yours in Christ Jesus.

Principle:
Christians can live expectantly
even in the dark times of life.

Christians who live expectantly in the comfort of God's love for them, with their hope set in heaven, can glorify God even in the midst of suffering. Dark times are an opportunity to be drawn deeper into the love and glory of God.

Are there ever times when health conditions or suffering are the consequence of sin? Yes, sometimes. When we abuse our bodies, ignore God's laws, and refuse to be good stewards of our bodies, we can suffer consequences. However, many times, physical suffering is hereditary or the result of living in a fallen world. Certainly God does not want us to berate ourselves for health conditions we suffer. He does want us, however, to be good stewards of our bodies! Were it not for the dark years the woman suffered, we would not be able to witness Jesus' power in her life.

Dark times are an opportunity to be drawn deeper into the love and glory of God.

Apply God's Word
If you have been told that you have an incurable disease or condition, what is your hope?

What testimony of Christ's love and provision in a time of suffering, darkness, or illness can you give?

How might Christ's glory shine through you in an area where you are currently experiencing darkness, weakness, or suffering?

Up Close and Personal

If you suffer guilt or shame from a prior sin, would you use this time to objectively think through the feelings you are experiencing? Fact: If your condition is caused by sin, God forgives you. You need not ask forgiveness repeatedly, but one time, in sincerity and honest confession. Come clean with God. Admit the error of your ways, acknowledge your sin, and ask God to forgive you on the basis of His mercy, not your goodness. Do it now.

If you have never viewed a chronic condition, time of weakness, or dark time as an opportunity for Christ's love and glory, would you consider how God might want to draw you close in His love and show His glory through you?

A Prayer Opportunity

God moves us beyond the basic first steps of our faith to deeper spiritual lessons as we walk and mature with Him. A challenging spiritual reality is that God allows us to suffer so that His love, glory, and power might abound in us. What do you need to pray about in relation to this lesson? (You may want to pray one of the Scriptures from Romans 8:18–39. For instance, "Lord, help me overwhelmingly conquer through You," Romans 8:37.)

Day Three
Faith and Hope Come by Hearing

Mark 5:25–29

Lord, today, please convict and convince us that faith comes by hearing. Convict and convince us that we should be messengers of Your grace and hope! Let this woman's suffering serve as an example to us. May the fact that her life remains a model to us more than two thousand years after she lived inspire us to be messengers of the hope found in You. Amen.

When the advice of doctors and medical treatments do not help, what can you do? Bonnie Frantzen, a longtime friend and Bible study leader, and her daughter, Hailey, are examples of God's glory abounding in the midst of illness. Two years ago, Hailey began having health problems and since then has been to a number of doctors, trying to get a correct diagnosis and cure. Recently, I received an email from Bonnie, a portion of which I share with you below.

Dear Friends,
We went back to the doctor today. After all the testing and elimination of possibilities we know it is not Crohn's or Celiac disease. The doctor is researching a new treatment and will let us know something when we go back in three months. We were told that she is in pretty good shape compared to some patients who have feeding tubes. Praise the Lord for this! We just need prayers that her condition does not worsen. She can live with her condition if it remains as it is. It may be like this all her life, but she is spunky and enjoys her life and has many interests that keep her and me busy.

The other prayer request is that she has turned into quite a beautiful singer and does quite a lot of public speaking. The continuous vomiting is not good for her. Please pray for protection for her voice and throat.

Again, thank you for all the emails, phone calls, and especially your prayers. We could not have made it without you. The Lord has taught us many things. For myself, I do not order the steps of my day,

God does. And He loves me very much and is teaching me about compassion. I know Hailey has learned about keeping on through adversities. Many life lessons to take with her in her walk with the Lord.

Love,
Bonnie

When I read Bonnie's email, my heart filled with emotions. Sorrow for Hailey and her discomfort flooded me; then amazement as Bonnie reported Hailey to be spunky and enjoying life . . . amidst vomiting, inability to eat normally, and sickness. Bonnie, doing whatever she needed one day at a time for Hailey and learning compassion, touched me. Hailey challenges my faith by not giving up on life, but speaking and singing in the midst of a condition that causes her to vomit and harm her throat! Are you touched as I am? Do this mother and daughter bless you?

God uses people like Bonnie and Hailey, who are not healed, but live by God's power in the midst of their present illness. Not everyone is healed. Sometimes we are called to live with our weaknesses, disabilities, and suffering. If you are that person or one caring for someone in that condition, how are you doing?

There were times when I cared for my mother that I would have had to honestly answer that question, "Not very well." There were times when I thought I could not handle the responsibilities God put before me. I hated seeing Mama hurt. I could not stand the times she suffered in pain. I felt deeply for her when she wished she could stop taking all her medicine and injections; when she suffered with infections, glaucoma, kidney failure, congestive heart failure, ambulance runs to the emergency room in the wee hours of the morning, and finally death by ovarian cancer.

Mother and my sisters, Vicki and Linda, years earlier cared for our father, who had Alzheimer's. Apart from God's grace, they could not have managed the 36-hour days. Cruelly, disease often ravages the body and mind of those we love. How the sick person and the caregiver weather the seasons of life and disease differs according to one's faith, hope, and perseverance.

Where are you on the continuum of perseverance, faith,

God uses people like Bonnie and Hailey.

and hope in regard to a physical condition you or a loved one suffer? How can we be better stewards of our bodies, minds, and emotions, knowing that loved ones may need to care for us one day? How can we move from anger to peace, from resentment to love, from hopelessness to hope, and from faithlessness to faithfully being an instrument of God's glory? Today's lesson will give us insight!

Read Mark 5:25–29. What was the condition of the woman with the hemorrhage? Check all that are true.
❏ **She had been to many physicians.**
❏ **She had spent all that she had.**
❏ **She was not helped at all.**
❏ **She had grown worse.**

At this point, if you were the woman, how would you be feeling?
❏ **Desperate**
❏ **Lonely**
❏ **Hopeful**
❏ **Hopeless**

Hopelessness is a major contributor to depression and suicide. Dawn McMullan, in her article "Matters of Life and Death," in the July 2003 edition of the *Baylor Magazine*, gives the following statistics on suicide.

- 80 people a day commit suicide—one person every 18 minutes.
- 29,350 people committed suicide in the United States in 2000.
- There are an estimated 734,000 suicide attempts in the United States annually; for every 25 attempts there is one death.
- Five million Americans have tried to kill themselves.
- Twice as many deaths result from suicide as from AIDS.
- Suicide is the 11th leading cause of death and the 3rd leading cause of death in people ages 10 to 24.
- In the past three decades, the number of suicides committed by people ages 15 to 24 has tripled.

Science alone will not stop suicides. "Values, belief systems, and philosophies of living make a difference. Hope makes a difference," states Dr. M. David Rudd, president of the American Association of Suicidology and professor of

Hope makes a difference.

psychology and neuroscience at Baylor University. He continues, "Although the common method of treating suicidal patients today is through the insight model, which seeks to gain perspective by focusing on one's past, the emerging method of treatment is the cognitive model, which teaches people how to respond and react in healthier ways,"

In studying suicide notes of people who attempted or actually committed suicide, Dr. Rudd identified four cognitive themes:

• Unlovability
• Helplessness
• Poor distress tolerance
• Perceived burdensomeness

Principle:
Christians have cognitive tools to teach others
how to respond and react in dire situations.

Some readers may be thinking, "What tools?" Perhaps many of us are like the person who receives a gift of tools. We stare at the numerous sizes and shapes of the tools, not having any idea how to use them. When our car breaks down on a deserted road, we know we have tools in our trunk, but do not know how to use them.

Often people are excited when they receive Christ and begin to read their Bible. But when illness strikes, marital discord occurs, a rebellious child strikes out, or unmanageable bills pile in, they look at their Bible thinking, "Surely the answer is in here," but they do not know where to find the answer. If you are a Christian who is familiar with the tools in God's Word, please use them, rather than tinker around! Be a demonstration of how to apply the tools of God! If you are a Christian who is less mature in the faith, please do not stop seeking biblical tools to use in dire situations!

The good news and the beauty of the account of Mark 5:21–27 is found in Mark 5:27. **Check the following facts about the woman with the hemorrhage.**
❑ **She accidentally found Jesus.**
❑ **Someone told her about Jesus.**
❑ **She had renewed hope after hearing about Jesus.**

There are many facts we do not know about this woman. We do not know if she was married or unmarried, if she had children, or what her moral or spiritual condition was. This is encouraging for one who thinks Jesus is only for a set group of religious people. The point of the story is one woman in need came to Jesus because she heard about Him, and He met her at her point of need.

God's Word has truths that can be tools in people's lives. Do you know someone who has any of the following thoughts?

- Unlovability ("I'm worthless.")
- Helplessness ("I can't solve my problems.")
- Poor distress tolerance ("I can't stand the way I feel.")
- Perceived burdensomeness ("Everyone would be better off if I were dead.")

I am disappointed in myself and my life. Romans 10:11

I have no hope. Romans 15:13

I have so much sin and guilt in my life! Romans 10:9–10

I can't pray. Romans 8:26–27

Nothing good can ever come from my life. Romans 8:28

No one is for me. Everyone is against me. Romans 8:31–32

I have nothing to cling to. Romans 12:9

I have no one to live for, nothing to give to others. No one needs me. Romans 12:11, 13

I have nothing to be happy about. Romans 12:12

I'm going to treat him just as badly as he's treated me! Romans 12:14

In the end, when it is all said and done, God cares about the one in a dire situation. His Word has tools that can help us.

God cares about the one in a dire situation.

Apply God's Word

Considering the statistics for suicide, how important do you think it is for you to fulfill your obligation to God to take His Word and ways to others?

How might being more spiritually tuned to God and others be a blessing to both yourself and others?

Who needs to hear a word of God from you so that their faith and hope might grow, even as the woman heard and was led to seek Jesus?

Up Close and Personal

God's Word, the Bible, has many tools to repair broken hearts and ways of thinking. **What is God asking you to apply in your own life and in relation to others?**

1. In relation to my life:

2. In relation to others:

A Prayer Opportunity

Who could you speak to today so that they might be encouraged by what they hear? Use today's prayertime to ask God to help you find a way and the words to encourage someone today. Ask God to help you be more driven to His Word so you are better equipped with tools for daily living.

Day Four

A Memorable Spiritual Moment

Mark 5:25–30

Father, we rejoice when we read Your Word and see the beauty, the magnificence of Your power. We rejoice when we read how one woman reached out and touched You and in seeking You found power for her life! We yearn for Your power. May we not only yearn, but also reach out and touch You as she did! May Your power go forth in us. In Jesus' name, Amen.

When nothing works, not medication, doctor's advice, nor friend's suggestions, what can we do?

We can seek Jesus. We can acknowledge biblical truths. We can learn from the Bible healthy ways to respond to dire times in our life. We can find hope and encouragement by seeking Jesus and finding His power to be sufficient in our weakness.

The woman in our study is seeking. Today's account of her finding the answer in Jesus brings glory to God. Imagine the smile on the heavenly Father's face when she touched Jesus! One more daughter healed! One more daughter found His Son!

The synagogue official's daughter was important. But the woman with the hemorrhage was also important. So are you!

Once again, our heavenly Father wants to smile when we touch the power of His Son. Once again, Jesus wants to look and see the one who is seeking Him in prayer and reaching for His righteousness.

We will physically embrace Jesus when we see Him face to face. We will kiss His feet. For the present, though, He invites us to touch Him through prayer, His Word, and the Holy Spirit. On our knees, we can be affected by Christ's power. Won't you reach out and touch Him today?

Read Mark 5:25–30. What did this woman have to pay Jesus? Mark 5:26

On our knees, as the woman was, we can be affected by Christ's power.

What did she have to give Him?

What did Jesus require of her before He would help her?

Sometimes we may feel that we are not good enough or worthy to come to Jesus. Was this woman worthy in the eyes of others?
❏ Yes
❏ No

Did Jesus seem to mind that she was "unclean" when she touched His priestly tassel?
❏ No
❏ Yes

The woman without a cure came in weakness and brokenness to Jesus. Perhaps this is the first principle we need to understand if we desire to live in and be changed by God's power. Yet it is often in our most miserable state we feel the most unworthy to approach Jesus. We may feel unclean, unworthy. Have you ever felt that way? Is it true? Is it a valid thought? Or is it, in fact, when we are most needy God is able to help us?

When we have tried everything to be good, to do good, to find help, to be helped, and there is nothing at the end of the road except the face of Jesus, may we reach for Him, even if it is only for His tassel! May we not listen to the voice of Satan or anyone else who would stand in the way of our seeking Jesus and His power in our lives!

How did this woman come to Jesus? Mark 5:27
❏ Up to Him, face to face.
❏ Behind Jesus, to His back.

What was she thinking? Mark 5:28

Which of the following is sound biblical thinking? Check all that apply.

❏ Jesus is the One I can seek in any situation.
❏ I must become perfect, or at least better, before I go to Jesus.

The fringe or tassels on the hem of Jesus' garment, referred to in Luke 8:44, was in keeping with Numbers 15:37–39. **What did God want His people to remember? Numbers 15:39**

Which of His commandments did the Lord want people to remember? Numbers 15:40

What was the ultimate purpose of the tassels, of looking at them and remembering the Lord's commandments? Numbers 15:40

What did the Lord know would be tempting for the people as they lived among those who did not honor God? Check all that are true. Numbers 15:39

❏ It would be tempting to not do His commandments.
❏ It would be tempting to follow after their hearts, not God's.
❏ It would be tempting to follow after their eyes, not God's ways.

What does God call it when we do not follow all His commandments, when we follow after our own hearts and eyes? Numbers 15:39

Rather than be harlots, what does the Lord want us to be? Numbers 15:40

> **Principle:**
> **The Lord is in the business of transforming us from harlotry to holiness!**

Jesus wore the tassels. For those who dismiss the Old Testament, I encourage you to consider that Jesus is the fulfillment of the Old Testament. See Matthew 5:17. Rather than take the position that the Old Testament is obsolete, may we remember Jesus' teaching that not one part, not one jot of the Bible should be annulled (Matthew 5:18–20).

Jesus is the perfect fulfillment of the law. His righteousness brings judgment to earth. Yet at the same time, Jesus invites us to be forgiven of their sins through faith in Him.

If you have never received forgiveness for your sins, if you have felt removed from the law of God, may you see with renewed passion the purpose and plan of God for your life. Jesus came to lift you out of any miry clay that holds you in sin. He will cleanse you, just as you are. He will position you in heaven with your name recorded there forever. He will give you His Holy Spirit to help you.

Jesus came to lift us out of the miry clay.

His Spirit, by the power of God and Word of Truth, will begin transforming your life. Transformation begins when we acknowledge that Jesus is Lord. Take the step toward Him. Lay hold of the tassel of His righteous power and be forgiven, cleansed, adopted into the family of God! Pray now and ask God to forgive you of your sin. Confess Jesus as Lord if you have never done so before!

The woman with the hemorrhage reached out. She reached out for Jesus' holy power and glory. You can, too! If you have not already done so, thank Him now.

> **Principle:**
> **Jesus is our hope of glory and power.**

The woman with the hemorrhage wanted something. **What were her thoughts? Mark 5:28**

She wanted to get well. Did she? **Record what happened to her. Mark 5:29**

What did Jesus perceive in Himself? Mark 5:30

In that memorable, spiritual moment, something happened to both Jesus and the woman! **Which of the following describes the timing of when the woman touched Jesus and was healed and when Jesus perceived the power go forth from Him? Mark 5:29–30**
❑ **Soon after**
❑ **Immediately**

Immediately, the flow of her blood was dried up. Immediately, Jesus perceived in Himself that power proceeded from Him. At the moment the woman reached out and touched Jesus, His power went forth!

Oh, how amazing it is when we slow down and ponder the truths and reality of God's Word! The moment we come in need and grasp hold of Christ in our prayertime, in our searching through Scripture, Christ's power proceeds forth to help us! Hallelujah! Praise the Lord!

Apply God's Word
Do you ever feel unworthy to go to Jesus because you are unclean, you have miserably failed again, or you think you and your situation are not as important as they should be to bother God?

Is the above reasoning biblically sound? If so, record in the space below where the Bible says that you cannot go to Jesus for the forgiveness of sin. (Hint: You will not find it!)

If your way of thinking is not taught in the Bible, would you

begin following what God does tell you, to pray without ceasing, to pray about everything, to confess your sins?

Up Close and Personal

1. In what way or area of your life do you need a touch from God today?

2. How are you seeking His touch?

3. Are you willing to walk the path the woman walked to find Jesus' power and touch in the various areas of your life?

4. What in your life shows that you are undaunted in your pursuit of God and Christ's power and touch on your life?

5. If doubts of despair or unworthiness suddenly come upon you, how will you stay on course, seeking Christ and His empowerment?

A Prayer Opportunity

When the woman laid hold of Jesus, Jesus' power flooded her and her issue of blood stopped. Are you ready for Jesus to flood your life with His love and glory? Express your prayers, the cry of your heart to God.

Day Five

Who Touched Me?

Mark 5:30–34, Luke 8:43–48

Lord, how exciting it is to know that You are aware when we reach out and touch You! May we find grace and peace in this study as we rejoice that You call us to You, the Lord Most High. We bless Your holy name. Amen.

Reaching out and touching someone is pervasive in our society. Sometimes the touch is wanted. Sometime it is not. Many in our country were overjoyed when the national "Do Not Call" registration was established. People who did not want calls from telephone solicitors were able to put their name on a list that protected them from being called. Thank God that He has not established a "Do Not Call" list of people He does not want to be interrupted by!

In today's lesson, we find that Jesus was not angry with the hemorrhaging woman who touched Him. Jesus welcomed her touch. But He was not satisfied with her private faith. He called her to give a public explanation.

Read Mark 5:30–34 and Luke 8:43–48. Jesus was headed to the home of Jairus, the synagogue official, whose daughter was near death. Needless to say, that would have been considered an emergency! A crowd gathered and walked along with Jesus toward their home. **However, when the woman touched Jesus and was healed, what did Jesus do? Mark 5:30**

Jesus did not continue to Jairus' home. Rather, Jesus stopped and asked the most amazing question. **What question did Jesus ask? Mark 5:30**

The disciples, who often speak thoughts we might have had, asked a question that shows how strange they thought His question was. **What did they ask Jesus? Mark 5:31**

How many people admitted they had touched Jesus? Luke 8:45
❏ **None**
❏ **Several**

No one admitted they had touched Jesus. Yet what do we know the crowd had been doing? Luke 8:45

The people had been crowding and pressing in on Jesus. The reaction of the crowd is quite interesting. Although they pressed Jesus on every side, when He turned and asked, "Who touched Me?" they fell silent. They denied they had touched Him as if they feared His reaction to being pressed. Rather, Jesus was seeking to look into the eyes of the one He had healed.

Jesus sought the public profession for three reasons. First, Jesus desired intimacy with the woman and before the eyes of the witnesses. As a bride and groom publicly declare their love for one another in the presence of others, so Jesus desired to look this woman in the eyes, to acknowledge her worth and His love for her. He waited to see if she would come forth and acknowledge Him, whom she had sought and by whom she had been healed.

Second, Jesus' acknowledgment of her validated her health and wholeness in the eyes of all the people. The church is people who have sought and been changed by Jesus. The church is not perfect people. It is people who depend on the perfect Lord for their salvation.

Jesus did not drop the question when the crowd denied touching Him. He pursued the one who had reached out to Him in faith. **What did Jesus say? Luke 8:46**

Jesus was aware that power had gone forth from Him. Among the many hands that touched Him, one desperate hand grappled in faith through the crowd. Jesus wanted to come face to face with the recipient of His power and love.

> ## Principle:
> **Jesus wants those changed by His power to come forth.**

Read Luke 8:47. The woman had wanted to be healed. She believed by touching Jesus she could be. But she did not want any attention to be drawn to her. Have you ever felt that way?

Was Jesus unkind to demand she come forward? Never!

> Jesus was seeking to look in the eyes of the one He had healed.

Jesus' commands have purpose beyond our understanding, but they are always in our best interests. **When the woman saw that she had not escaped being noticed, what did she do? Divide Luke 8:47 into several points.**

1.

2.

3.

4.

The word *fear* in Mark 5:33 is the Greek word *phobeonai*, which means "to have awe and reverence." The woman moved forward through the crowd, trembling in awe of Jesus. We can imagine the crowd moving aside to let her pass as Jesus gazed into her eyes.

No longer hiding, she fell in reverence, bowing before the Son of God. In a trembling voice she declared in the presence of all the people the reason why she touched Jesus and how she had been immediately healed. To God goes the glory! The woman shared 1) her condition before she was healed, 2) how she came to Jesus, and 3) her condition after being changed by Jesus. **From what we have studied, what might she have said?**

Before today I was:

How I came to Jesus:

Since I touched Him, I:

The woman could have timidly said from the midst of the crowd, "I touched You." But she did not. She understood Christ was calling her. This was a moment for confession, worship, and sealing her experience in the eyes of God and before all the people. As hard as it was for her to come forward, it was a moment for her to be wonderfully released from her past and ushered into the presence of God's glory.

Jesus did not let this moment pass. The Master had healed

her. They had a relationship. Her value and healing were validated. She was restored in the community.

The call to public disclosure of our relationship with Jesus should extend beyond the walls of the church where believers gather. Public disclosure of Christ's glory and power should extend to where the crowds are. Others need to see and hear how Jesus can change our life.

Instantaneously, Jesus and the woman were face to face. **He called her something. What was it? Luke 8:48**

Daughter, a term of endearment and family acknowledgment, is used by Jesus only in this passage. The third reason Jesus sought the woman to publicly profess her faith was so He could build on the faith of the woman and the listening crowd. **What did Jesus teach her and, therefore, others? Luke 8:48**

Jesus explained that touching the tassel on His garment was not what healed her, lest any rest their faith on a thing. Rather, it was her faith that healed her.

Jesus' statement, "Go in peace," assured her that her healing was complete. In her extremity of need, incurable illness, and socio-religious isolation, she had been a living "dead" person for 12 years. As noted by John Grassmick in the *Bible Knowledge Commentary*, her restoration to wholeness of life anticipated the dramatic raising of Jairus' daughter who died after living for 12 years.

Not all of us will experience healing from chronic conditions in this life. As people continue to live longer, more people live with incurable conditions. Anger and bitterness can accompany pain and discomfort. One may wonder why she is not healed when another person is healed.

When nothing works, not healthy foods and drinks, medications, or treatment, what can we do?

We can seek Jesus as the ultimate answer to our dilemma.

We can place our faith in Jesus for the outcome, whether it is for deliverance from our condition or deliverance to live with our condition.

We can go to Jesus in prayer and experience the flow of His power in our life to live and walk in the works He has prepared for us.

We can declare before others what Jesus is doing for us.

We can follow the advice of health care professionals to which God leads us.

Principle:
In touching Jesus,
we can receive power for daily living.

Celebrate, dear friends! Celebrate, because in this lifetime or the next, by faith we will be made whole! We will see Jesus and worship at His feet!

Apply God's Word

The woman with the hemorrhage was called before Jesus to publicly confess what Jesus had done for her. Each of us who have come to Christ for salvation has a story. Here is the story of my salvation.

Before I became a Christian:
I knew Jesus through what others told me.

How I came to know Jesus personally, face to face:
In desperation I acknowledged that there was nothing good in me. I was a sinner bound to sin and eternity apart from God. I confessed to God and asked Him to forgive me and come into me.

Since coming to Jesus:
Christ dwells in me through His Holy Spirit. We are connected. I do not just know *about* Him, I know Him! I experience Jesus' love, power, and blessings in my life. I no longer try to struggle to live by His commandments. I live by His indwelling power, Christ in me. I still sin. I have sin habits that are strong. But God as my Father is disciplining me. Jesus as my Friend intercedes for me. The Holy Spirit as my Counselor comforts, guides, convicts, and conforms me to God's will, slowly, day by day. I am glad God is my Father, Jesus is my Friend, and the Holy Spirit is my Counselor. I have new life in Christ.

1. What is the story of your confession of faith in Jesus?
Before you became a Christian:

How you came to know Jesus personally, face to face:

Since you have been saved:

Each of us who have come to Christ for salvation has a story. But the testimony of our life does not end with our salvation. It is but the beginning! Our life should be a continuing testimony of how Christ is changing us.

Up Close and Personal

1. The woman we have studied this week was at the end of her rope. She heard about Jesus and went to Him in desperation. Perhaps you are in a desperate situation. Perhaps you have never come to Jesus personally but have just heard about Him. Or you may be the caregiver of one in pain. What is your situation?

2. Whether the situation you face is physical, spiritual, emotional, or financial, Jesus has the answer. The Scripture says that if you seek God, He will let you find Him. Seeking is not a one-time effort, but an ongoing prevailing attitude of heart and mind. Are you seeking?

3. Seeking implies opening up your heart in devotion and prayer, poring over God's Word to discover His ways. Seeking requires quietness so that the Spirit of God can

flow in and through you as a surge of electricity. **Seeking implies remaining** while the heavens open up and, like rain, pour forth the Holy Spirit's power, refreshing your barren soul. Are you seeking?

A Prayer Opportunity

Use this time to seek Christ's touch on your life and situation.

Week Four
Thinking It Over

Please look back over your lesson and prayerfully complete the following.

1. What was most meaningful to you in your study of this woman from:

Day 1

Day 2

Day 3

Day 4

Day 5

2. How did God stir and prompt your heart and mind by her story?

3. In what specific way does God want you to take care of your health, knowing that one day someone will take care of you?

4. How is this lesson calling you to speak of your faith so others in dire situations can hear the good news of Christ's power?

5. What "golden nugget" of truth do you want to remember from this week?

6. What verse do you want to remember from this week's lesson?

7. What is the prayerful cry of your heart in relation to this week's study?

Week Five

A Diseased Heart

Day One
Martha
Luke 10:38–42, John 11:1–44, 12:1–8

An ill-willed heart may not show itself in a diseased physical condition, but rather in a diseased relational condition with God and others.

Father, if our heart is darkened in any way against You or another, or clogged by misplaced priorities, please open the floodgate of our heart and wash us. Purify us and set our priorities in place. Overwhelm us with a passion for You. Amen.

As I stared at the stain on the carpet, I could not believe what I had done. Never had I seen such a huge, black, rusty, mildewed stain. I found it when Keith lifted a large plant for me to vacuum under. For months I had been watering the plant, not realizing there was a hole in the container, not realizing what

damage was happening underneath the beautiful green foliage.

I scrubbed, sprayed, dabbed, and pressed the ugly stain for an hour and a half. As I sat and pondered it, I could not help but think how God must view my sin. To Him, the petty comments, unkind remarks, and lack of discipline must rust away at the heart I ask Him to fill. I thank God that He does not let me remain in my sin, but rather presses on the dark sin spots of my heart. I am thankful that, in love, He washes me with His Holy Spirit.

God presses and convicts those He loves. Today He cleans Christians through His Holy Spirit and the Word. When Jesus walked on earth, He spoke directly to people when He saw the sin in their heart beneath their service and words.

One such person Jesus pressed was Martha. He responded to her about an area that was rusting away at her heart of service and hospitality.

As we study this week, we want to consider:

1. Is there a sin in my life that may not be obvious to others, but Jesus sees?
2. Is it eating away at my health, my walk with God, or my relationship with another person?
3. What is God pressing me about concerning my priorities and passions?

Read Luke 10:38–42. This is a wonderful account of Jesus sitting in the home of three friends, enjoying an evening at "home." The village referred to in Luke 10:38 is Bethany, located on the eastern slope of the Mount of Olives, about two miles from Jerusalem. A small village, a home of two sisters and a brother . . . blessed by Jesus. These were good folks! The more we study them this week, the more you will like them. There was nothing pretentious about Martha, Mary, and Lazarus. Jesus enjoyed being with them.

Reread Luke 10:38. Who was the first person to greet Jesus at the door and welcome Him into her home?

What was Martha's sister's name?

Where do we find Mary seated?

What was Mary doing?

We can picture Mary sitting at the feet of Jesus, captivated and clinging to every word He spoke. Several years ago, Dan Yeary, pastor of North Phoenix Baptist Church in Arizona, preached at our church. We were honored and excited when he came to our home one night after the worship service. I had prepared Taylor and Lauren, who were young at the time, to sit quietly and listen to every word this fine man of God spoke. To have Dan Yeary accept the invitation into our home was an honor.

Mary seemed to grasp the honor of having Jesus in her home. But how is Martha described? See Luke 10:40.
❏ **Determined to spend time with Jesus**
❏ **Distracted**

Who was Martha distracted from?
❏ **Jesus**
❏ **The crowds**

What distracted Martha from Jesus? Luke 10:40–41

Martha was distracted from Jesus by all her preparations and by things! What a sad statement of condition! Could it be said of us?

> ## Principle:
> **To be distracted from Jesus by things
> is a sad statement of condition!**

Mary and Martha are going to make future actions that are in keeping with their present choices. We are going to see their decisions and lives unfold before us. As we do, pay careful attention to each woman. Choose which type of woman you want to be.

Where is Jesus, the Son of God? Seated, sharing His heart. If you have ever heard a truly spirit filled preacher or friend speak, you recognize their words are not merely scriptural

See and choose which type of woman you want to become.

knowledge. You sense the Spirit of God and want to sit and listen.

You want to sit and listen unless you are too busy.

I do not believe Martha would have intentionally discounted the Lord's presence or words in any way to anyone. I believe she would have defended Him to anyone.

So why did she choose not to sit with Him? How is it that Mary recognized Jesus' need to eat, but upon His arrival chose to sit at His feet?

Reread Luke 10:40. Where was Martha?
❑ **At Jesus' feet**
❑ **Distracted from Jesus with all *her* preparations**

What did Martha decide to do about Mary not pitching in and helping?
❑ **She went to Mary and quietly asked her to help.**
❑ **She went to Jesus and complained about Mary to Him.**

What did Martha accuse Jesus of?
❑ **Not caring that Mary had left her to do all the serving.**
❑ **Bringing so many disciples to eat without telling her beforehand.**

What did Martha tell Jesus to do about the situation?

Ouch! This is hitting too close to home! I can see myself wanting everything to be just right for Jesus. I would want the food to taste yummy and the presentation to be honoring to the Lord. I would expect my sister to help me, not just sit on the floor.

Read closely Luke 10:41. Can you hear Jesus tenderly saying, "Martha, Martha"? He knew her name. He recognized her worth. But . . .

Fill in the blanks with Jesus' perspective of Martha.
You are _____.

You are bothered about so many _____.

Jesus looked at Martha and saw the situation for what it was.

He saw her heart and counseled, "You are worried and bothered about so many things."

Might Jesus say your name, call attention to your value, but then counsel you as He did Martha, "You are worried and bothered by so many things?" We might want to retort, "Well somebody has to be!" We might think, even if we did not voice it, "There are a lot of things to worry about!"

Notice Martha's silence. Jesus says something of great value to her, to all of us.

Read Luke 10:42. What does Jesus tell Martha?
Only _____ thing is _____.

> ### Principle:
> **Only one thing is necessary.**

I wonder how many "things" in my life Jesus looks at and considers unnecessary. "Things" distract us. "Things" bother us. "Things" press us on every side. They pressed in on Jesus, too. However, Jesus managed to find balance and peace in the midst of the crowds, healings, attempts on His life, quarreling disciples, interrupting family members, and teaching responsibilities.

What was His secret? One thing. In the movie, *City Slickers*, Jack Palance, who played the seasoned trail cowboy, told city slicker Billy Crystal that only one thing mattered. The city slicker determined to discover what the one thing was that mattered most in his life.

Do you wonder, as you read this passage, "What is the one necessary thing?" **Read Luke 10:42 and see if you can determine what necessary thing Martha missed but Mary grasped. Consider Jesus' words as words for you as you record them below.**

Why does Jesus say the two women responded as they did?
❏ **They were genetically disposed the way they were.**
❏ **Their parents had treated them differently.**
❏ **They chose.**

> ## Principle:
> We can choose the good part of life . . .
> to sit and worship at Jesus' feet.

Jesus makes a statement about the "good part."

Read Luke 10:42. What are Jesus' conclusive words and actions? Check True or False.
True False

- ❏ ❏ Martha's service would live on into eternity.
- ❏ ❏ Mary's intimacy at Jesus feet would not be taken away from her.

Apply God's Word

Martha was distracted from Jesus by all *her* preparations *for* Him. **In what ways do you prepare "things" such as Bible lessons, or meals for the sick, all for Jesus, yet you are distracted from His very presence, sitting at His feet, and listening to His words?**

How often do you have a worried, bothered, or martyred look on your face while you are doing things for the Lord such as taking your children to church, hosting a youth group, or tending to your husband's or another person's needs?

How would you describe the one thing in life that is necessary, that which Mary chose and Martha did not choose?

Up Close and Personal

Today, many women are distracted and bothered by so many things that they are stressed and sleep deprived. Lack of sleep and exercise, poor eating habits, and not taking care of our bodies can result in anxious, tired countenances, short fuses, and, ultimately, medical problems.

We may pray for patience, love, joy, and health, but if we are deprived of sleep and vital nutrients, and time with Jesus, we may be fighting a losing battle. The battle, when turned over to the Lord, can be won. **If God could take something out of your life that you are bothered and distracted by, what would it be? (Children and spouses not included!)**

The battle, when turned over to the Lord, can be won.

Many women work at least two full-time jobs. They work or volunteer outside the home and they work at home. There is little or no time for rest, proper care for their body, and being with family, and much less time to "sit at Jesus' feet." **Are the things you are involved with truly necessary? Record your thoughts on the basis of Jesus' summary of Martha's situation. Luke 10:42**

Many parents work hard to give their children more material advantages. The trade-off is that sometimes children get less of what they really need: parents at home, teaching them about God, guiding them in the ways of Jesus. Often family members do not care for their aging parents, but rather leave it up to strangers because they are too busy, when what our loved ones really need is our caring touch and time.

What would it mean, in light of eternity, if you were not bothered by so many things and had more time to sit at Jesus' feet and then serve Him, caring for those He has entrusted to you?

What would it mean in terms of your relationship with God and others if you rested, ate properly, exercised, and worshipped at Jesus' feet?

A Prayer Opportunity

I am thankful that Jesus lets us pray to Him about what is on our minds and hearts. Certainly, Jesus does not fault any of us for doing what we need to do to take care of financial needs. Many single parents have no choice but to work outside the home. God's Word applauds the Proverbs 31 woman who rises early while it is still dark and works outside her home as well as in her home. Where we work is not so much the question, as where our priorities are. Sitting at Jesus' feet and listening to His Words seems to be non-negotiable in this passage, for that is the good part of life, the eternal part. Pray about what is on your mind in relation to today's lesson.

Day Two

So God May Be Glorified
John 11:1–44

Lord, how we praise You! In Your creation, we see Your handiwork. In the sun shining through the clouds, we worship. In the setting of the sun, we are reminded of Your faithfulness to us today. Oh, how You bless us with Your presence though we are unworthy. May we bless You now by tuning our ears to Your words and our hearts to Your heart. Amen.

Martha revealed something in her heart that was dark. Others might not have seen it, but it is likely that they did. She was serving, but her heart was far from Jesus. Our heart is where our body is, and many Americans have stressed hearts. Problems and priorities are not being laid at Jesus' feet. We often do not prioritize our lives by seeking first the kingdom of God and listening to Jesus. Listening takes time. Prayer is not just about giving Jesus a to-do list, as Martha did. It is about listening to Jesus' responses in regard to our concerns. Do you have a place to go and a time set aside to sit a Jesus' feet?

Listening takes time.

In today's study, we continue to follow Martha's life. We will be impressed with her confession of faith. **Read John 11:1–44. I hope you have time to read all of it in one sitting. If not, focus on John 11:1–4.**

In this passage we are reacquainted with three family members. **Who are they? List them in the order in which their names appear, and what they are known for. John 11:1–2**

Name   How Known

Did you find you needed more space to write about Mary? Why do you think that is? What made Mary's life remarkable?

Ponder this point in relation to your own life. Would there be much to remark on about you?

Mary is remembered for her relationship with Jesus. What she did for Him, with Him, at His feet is memorable. **What about Martha?**

Read John 11:2–3. What was the problem?

Who did the sisters send word to?

What do you think they expected, considering His love for Lazarus?

Read John 11:4–6. Did Jesus come quickly?
❏ Yes
❏ No

The word *love* in verse 3, referring to Jesus' feelings toward Lazarus, is the Greek word *phileo* and connotes the idea of

friendship and cordially liking a person. It often involves a shared interest or commitment to a common cause or to cherished ideals.

Jesus loved and enjoyed Lazarus. One would have expected Jesus to come sooner rather than later, to not wait even one day, much less four days.

How did Jesus respond when He received Martha and Mary's message? John 11:4

In John 11:5 we are told how Jesus felt about Martha and Mary, as well as Lazarus. **What word is used to describe Jesus' feelings toward them?**

Interestingly, the word *loved* in this verse is different from the word *love* in verse 3. The word *loved* in verse 5 is the Greek word *agape* and refers to an unselfish, outgoing affection or tenderness without necessarily expecting anything in return. *Agape* denotes a self-giving commitment irrespective of grateful response. Why is this important? Why is there a need to affirm Jesus' love for Martha, Mary, and Lazarus in the midst of His words in verse 4 and His decision in verse 6?

Principle:
Jesus' love for us sometimes requires He not respond immediately or in the way we want Him to for the highest good to be accomplished.

Agape seeks a person's highest good. Have you ever questioned why Jesus did not respond the way you wanted, when you knew He loved you, your child, your spouse, or another? God's silences are difficult. At times we may ask why.

I pray that through this week our faith can be renewed and increased. I pray that we can let go of any hurt or anger we have harbored toward God because we did not understand why things happened as they did. May we release any disbelief and trust God's sovereignty. If you need time for prayer, use this time now.

> **Principle:**
> Jesus loved Martha, Mary, and Lazarus.
> Jesus loves you and your loved ones.

Reread John 11:4. God allows some things we do not understand for the glory of God. How could Lazarus' death be for the glory of God? How did Jesus decide how many days to wait? Was He tired or uncaring? Was He preoccupied where He was? I am thankful that it was more than a random decision when Jesus would go to Bethany. Many factors were involved, but the most important element that affected Jesus' timing and the events that followed is found in John 11:7–10.

Read John 11:7–10. Think of the times you have had to make decisions. How many times have you not known which way to go?

Although we may analyze the pros and cons of a decision, it does not always help. The columns may be even! **Record the pros and cons of Jesus returning to Judea. John 11:3–16**

	Pros	Cons
verse 3		
verse 8		
verse 11		
verse 14		
verse 15		
verse 16		

What is the key to making decisions, to walking in God's will? Read John 11:9–11. What is Jesus teaching?

The teaching in this passage is that if we walk in the light of the Spirit we will not stumble. We will make decisions according to His will. But if we walk apart from the light of Christ we will stumble, because we walk in darkness. Enlightenment comes from God, His Word, and the Holy Spirit.

When we make decisions outside the will of God, apart

God allows some things we do not understand for the glory of God.

Enlightenment comes from God, His Word, and the Holy Spirit.

from prayer, we may rightly lack confidence. We may fear what looms ahead. Jesus demonstrated being divinely guided to go to Judea although there was a death threat against Him, because God directed His steps.

Principle:
Confidence accompanies our decisions
when we walk by the Spirit.

How did Jesus know what to do and when? Jesus spent time in prayer. Jesus followed the Spirit's leading. Jesus obeyed God's commandments.

Apply God's Word
John 11:4 teaches us that God allows some things we do not understand, for the glory of God. **What is your testimony regarding this? When have you found this to be true?**

Obeying God's commandments, prayer, and following the Holy Spirit's leading takes a lot of guesswork out of life. **Which of the three do you need to develop in your spiritual walk?**

Up Close and Personal
The disciples tended to look at the outward appearance of circumstances and statements Jesus made. They tended to jump in with their comments, fears, and misunderstanding. They would have gone when they needed to wait. They would have stayed when they needed to go. When they went, they thought they were going to die. **In what ways do you tend to walk as the disciples . . . by sight?**

Consider how Jesus walked by the Spirit, in the light of God's Word and prayer. How is God calling you to be less sight- and stress-led and more Spirit-led?

A Prayer Opportunity

Reflect over today's study. What penetrated your heart? Would you consider how God is prompting and convicting you, trying to get your attention and heart? What is your response to Him?

Day Three

Do You Believe?

John 11:11–31

Heavenly Father, as we approach Your Word today, speak to our hearts! May we understand with renewed clarity that You are the Resurrection and Life! Amen.

We do not know the cause of Lazarus' sickness, but we do know that Martha suffered with a "bothered and worried" heart. Distraction from Jesus and a watchful eye on Mary caused the ebb and flow of what should have been joyful service to be constrained. Resentment and "things" built up in her like plaque in one's veins. Jesus, the Great Physician, went straight to the source of her problem. She suffered from a heart condition known as worldliness. Too many things bothered her and distracted her from the one thing that was really good—Jesus!

The Mayo Clinic's February 14, 2003, top health threats for women may be a surprise to you. Do you know what threatens your physical life the most? Heart disease.

Heart disease is responsible for more deaths in women than all forms of cancer combined. In fact, more women than men die of heart disease. The good news is that heart disease is one of the most preventable health conditions. You have the power to reduce some of your risks by:

- Avoiding smoking and limiting or avoiding alcohol
- Eating a diet rich in fruits, vegetables, and grain products
- Exercising regularly
- Controlling other health conditions that may put a strain on your heart, such as high blood pressure, diabetes, and high cholesterol

I have not always considered my eating habits and exercise as top priorities. I took time for the Lord, for my family, for ministry, but not time to exercise as much as I needed or to be as selective with my food choices as I should be. My attitude has changed. I have grown to understand that caring for my physical body is important, for with it I can serve the Lord. Understanding this principle is important!

We do not know the cause of Lazarus' illness or death. We do know that no matter how well we take care of our body, we will die one day. Jesus used Lazarus' death and resurrection to give a visual, spiritual teaching. Lazarus' resurrection gives proof of a bodily resurrection from the grave. In addition, it foreshadows Jesus' death, burial, and resurrection.

Read John 11:11–17. Why did Jesus say Lazarus had "fallen asleep"? John 11:11
❏ **Lazarus was sleeping.**
❏ **Lazarus was dead.**

Jesus used the metaphor "fallen asleep," to explain that Lazarus had died. He also used the term in Mark 5:39 in relation to a child already pronounced dead. The term *fallen asleep* is used in two other familiar New Testament passages.

Record the context in which it is used.

Acts 7:59–60

1 Thessalonians 4:13–14

The disciples thought Lazarus was merely asleep, so what did Jesus explain? John 11:14

How do you suppose Jesus knew Lazarus was dead?

What did Jesus say in John 11:15?

What was Jesus' chief goal, His main aim in the miracles He performed?
❑ To help people believe He was the Christ, the Son of the Living God.
❑ To gain a position on the Council.

Read John 11:17–27, a wonderful passage! How many days had Lazarus been dead and where was his body?

Apparently Lazarus died shortly after the messengers left, because it was a day's journey to Jesus beyond the Jordan (10:40). He stayed there two days and spent a day traveling back to Bethany. **As Jesus drew closer to Bethany, who went to meet Him?**

What did Martha do or say when she first saw Jesus? John 11:21

What belief in Jesus did she profess? John 11:22

What promise beyond all other comforts did Jesus make to Martha? John 11:23

Martha thought Jesus meant that Lazarus would rise in the resurrection, but that was not the resurrection He was referring to. **What great words did Jesus speak in John 11:25–26? Write out the verses.**

Jesus is here and is calling for you.

Think on Jesus' words. Meditate on them. Chew on them for a minute. Memorize them! How can a person live and never die? Charles Ryrie in the *Ryrie Study Bible* phrases Jesus' statement in the following, helpful way: *"everyone who lives* physically *and believes in Me will never die* spiritually and eternally."*

Martha makes a great profession of her faith at this time. Food does not matter. Serving is not an issue. It is just Martha and Jesus. Listen to the profound conversation they are having! Although it is unfortunate that it seems to require the death of a loved one for her to listen to Jesus, how wonderful that she is listening now! **What great profession of faith in Jesus does Martha make? (John 11:27) Interpret what Martha said in your own words, first person.**

Martha made a great profession of faith in Jesus, but do you believe she understood that Jesus was going to raise Lazarus from the dead in just a few moments? See John 11:39–40 for help with your answer.
❑ **Yes**
❑ **No**

After visiting with Jesus, Martha went to get Mary. **Read John 11:28–33.** How precious to know that Jesus called for Mary. Jesus had probably stayed a distance from the house so He could meet with Martha and Mary privately. He took precious moments to console them and be with them in their grief. **What was Mary's response to Jesus calling for her? John 11:29**

What did Mary do when she first saw Jesus?
❑ **Said, "Lord, if You had been here, my brother would not have died."**
❑ **Fell at Jesus' feet.**

Martha, who was always the first to greet Jesus, was in actuality behind Mary in terms of intimacy with Jesus. Mary demonstrated her intimacy with Jesus by her behavior, by being at Jesus' feet, and by her words. Martha professed her faith.

Mary lived it. What about your faith?

Apply God's Word
If you were standing before Jesus at this moment, as Martha stood before Him, and He said to you what He said to her in John 11:25–26, how would you reply?

Martha called Jesus "Teacher" and "Lord." How do Jesus' words in John 13:13–17 apply to you in regard to you calling Jesus "Teacher" and "Lord" of your daily walk?

Up Close and Personal
If you were sitting in the sanctuary of the church and someone came from a nearby room and whispered in your ear, "Jesus is here and is calling for you," how would you feel? What would race through your mind?

Martha professed her faith. Mary lived in intimacy with Jesus, at His feet. Who do you more resemble and in what way?

Are you at the church door, professing your faith, reciting Scripture, singing hymns and praises, but carrying a diseased heart? Or are you living at the feet of Jesus?

How is God calling you to choose the "good" part of life physically and spiritually?

Physically

Spiritually

When and for what reason have you most recently run and fallen at Jesus' feet?

Knowing that spiritual heart disease is the number one health threat to your spiritual life, check which of the following you need to give immediate attention to.

4 Top Spiritual Heart Threats to Christian Women
- ❑ 1. Carnality—being bothered, distracted by things rather than intimate with Jesus.
- ❑ 2. Grieving the Holy Spirit by sin.
- ❑ 3. Quenching the Holy Spirit by ignoring His promptings as one ignores physical symptoms of a heart attack.
- ❑ 4. Walking in the flesh, which presents itself in frustration, boredom, lack of joy, hopelessness, unrest, impaired decision-making, panic, fear, self-centeredness, gluttony, sexual sins, outbursts of anger, being envious, sorcery, drunkenness, lying, stealing.

A Prayer Opportunity
What is on your heart today? Will you pray about it? Will you also sit still and let Jesus speak to your heart about your spiritual and physical health?

Day Four
Lazarus, Come Forth!
John 11:32–44

Lord, You are the Resurrection and the Life! There is no one who can forgive our sins and clothe us with righteousness but You! You called Lazarus to come forth from the tomb by the power of Your might. May each of us hear Your voice to come forth from any sin that binds us. To You, Lord, we give glory, honor, and praise. In Jesus' Name, Amen.

Woman's World ran an article in June 2003 titled, "The 30-

Minute Weight-Loss Miracle That Will Change Your Life!" Why is it touted as a miracle? Because the women who were featured had been imprisoned in a body they did not want but could not free themselves of. Nothing worked for them until they joined Curves, a fitness center for women. To them, it was a miracle to break free from the body they had been enslaved to.

In our account today, there is a miracle beyond what any man or woman might do! Jesus performs a miracle that cannot be explained away. We have the opportunity to visit the site, to hear the conversations and witness the miracle for ourselves. **Read John 11:32–44.**

Picture the hilly terrain, the dusty roads, the mourners who have gathered to console Mary and Martha. Listen to their conversations. See the looks on their faces. **What caused Jesus to be deeply moved in spirit and troubled? John 11:32–33**

With Martha, we hear her profession. With Mary, we see passion. Jesus is tied up in her life and she is tied up in His. They shared a common love for Lazarus and when Jesus sees her, it brings forth His emotions. **The shortest verse in the English Bible is John 11:35. Record the verse in the space below.**

Two words say it all. Jesus wept. Jesus wept at the depravity and decay that sin brought upon man. He was going to raise Lazarus, but He still felt the sorrow of death. It is interesting to listen to the conversations of those in the crowd watching Jesus. **What were some of the Jews saying about Him? John 11:36**

What were others saying? John 11:37

There are always those who have a better way things can be done, and who love to talk among themselves about it. May we guard our hearts in that respect! When we want God to do something "yesterday," we might take care to wait patiently for what He is accomplishing in the interim. When we are

tempted to be critical of how God is accomplishing something, we might reconsider and turn our complaints into praise for His presence.

Jesus at the tomb, Jesus at the cave, Jesus before the stone, was deeply moved. Then, in the next moment, Jesus, Lord of Hosts, made a command. The Son of God gave a visual that would remain in the minds and hearts of those present and future. He did not just say He was the Resurrection and Life. He became the Resurrection and Life for Lazarus. Is He going to be yours? Have you put your faith in Jesus to call you from your tomb? If not, my friend, do not delay. We never know when our hour of death may come. **What did Jesus command? John 11:39**

According to Gleason Archer in *The Discovery Bible*, Jesus' command is emphatic! Jesus is not just contemplating what He wants done. He commands, "Do this! Make this happen! Don't just try! Begin to do this now!"

We can imagine the tenseness and restlessness in the crowd of mourners. Those hard of hearing may have whispered to a friend, "What did He say?" Shock must have been present on the faces of all! Did Mary stop weeping to look up in puzzlement and wonder?

Who speaks up?
❏ **Mary**
❏ **Martha**

Martha proceeds to tell Jesus, who moments before she professed to be "the Son of God," that He really does not want what He has commanded. Then she proceeds to explain to Jesus why His command is a bad idea!

"Lord," she prefaced her objection, "with all due respect, I know something that you do not know. Perhaps you are not aware that Lazarus has been dead for four days. Or maybe you are not aware that there will be a stench."

As I write this I am convicted that too many times I have done what Martha did. Jesus gives a command, and then I refuse on the basis of my logic. I call Jesus Lord, but then I argue with Him. I profess faith but when called on to participate in what He wants me to do, I back down. Perhaps

Jesus is smiling that He finally got through to me in the mirror of Martha.

What about you? Do you ever come up with objections to what God wants, what He commands in His Word, or to His ways? Do you not go to Him more often because you already have your plans? When you pray and ask God for direction and He gives it, do you follow in faith or back down in fear?

Martha had wanted Jesus to come to the rescue. Now He is present, and she is resisting Him. **Only minutes earlier, what had Martha said? John 11:22**

Yet now Jesus asks, or rather commands, cooperation in a miracle He is going to do and Martha is the first to object. "Give us a miracle, O Lord, we pray. Just do it a normal, comfortable way. And please don't ask our help or participation." The miracle was momentarily delayed. Lazarus stayed in the tomb while the Son of God responded to Martha. **What did Jesus say to her?**

Jesus is kind. He does not rebuke Martha. He does remind her of their prior conversation, of her profession of faith. **What is Jesus reminding you?**

Principle:
Professing our faith is easier than practicing our faith.

May we be careful to be practitioners of our faith as well as professors! Jesus desires that we not only talk the Christian talk, but that we walk the Christian walk. The glory of God is at stake at Bethany. Jesus told Martha she would see the glory of God if she believed. What is the glory of God? It is His manifest power to claim life over death, victory over defeat, freedom over enslavements, power over weakness.

Do you need a dose of the glory of God in your life? If so,

May we be careful to be practitioners of our faith as well as professors!

what does Jesus say to do?

❏ Work hard.
❏ Believe.

How does Colossians 1:27 further explain how the glory of God is experienced in the Christian's life?

Principle:
The glory of God is accomplished through Jesus' power in the believer.

Martha says nothing. She is quieted by Jesus. Jesus is going to resurrect Lazarus! The men obey Jesus' command. They roll the stone from the entrance of the cave where Lazarus lay dead. **Read John 11:41. What does Jesus do? Where are His eyes?**

Jesus' eyes are raised. He is not looking at the grave or the problem, but to His Father. Oh, may we learn from our Lord! The first words out of Jesus' mouth are "Father." Abba, Daddy.

The next words are words of request. True or False?
❏ True
❏ False

What does Jesus pray in John 11:41?

Read John 11:42. What reason does Jesus give for praying aloud to His Father?

Principle:
Jesus' purpose is to bring people to faith in Him, the
Son of God.

Jesus prays aloud so that those listening will believe! If we love Jesus and claim to be His followers, should we not have as our life purpose His life purpose? Like Father, like Son. Like Savior, like Christian? **Read John 11:43.**

Following Jesus' prayer, the mourners are shocked into the present by Jesus' next words and loud cry. **What does Jesus cry out with a loud voice?**

What do they see, to their amazement?

Jesus will do that for you one day! He will do it for your loved ones! The grave does not hold the Christian captive. **As a matter of fact, after Jesus' death, what happened? Matthew 27:50–53**

Read Luke 4:18–19, Jesus' words in which He announced His ministry. What did Jesus say the Spirit of the Lord was upon Him to do?

Jesus is who He said He was, did what He came to do, and is able to set you free. Martha, Mary, and the mourners must have stood frozen as Lazarus came forth from the tomb! **What does Jesus command the bystanders to do to Lazarus? John 11:44**

> Jesus is who He said He was. Jesus did what He came to do.

Jesus does not raise Christians to new life to remain bound in their pre-salvation sin bindings. Jesus calls us to resurrection life that we might walk freely in the new life He has given us. May we walk as resurrected women, free of sin's bindings! May we walk in the righteousness He has clothed us in. May

> Jesus calls us to resurrection life that we might walk as new men and women!

we help unbind others from their grave clothes so that they may walk in newness of life by the power of the Holy Spirit!

Come forth! Jesus calls! Come forth! Jesus commands! Only believe.

Apply God's Word

In what way do you need to guard against objecting to God's Word or ways on the basis of your lack of faith or fear as Martha did?

In what way do you need to act in faith and "roll some stones," in accordance with your profession of who Jesus is?

Up Close and Personal

How might you be missing God's best because you do not go to Jesus with problems—you assume things are dead, past, gone?

When you pray and ask God for direction and He gives it, how well do you follow through with what He impresses on your heart? Or, do you let fear or sin sidetrack you so that you stop short of His miracles?

In what area of your life is the "Teacher" teaching you and calling you to believe?

In what area might Jesus be grieved about unconfessed sin and its consequence in your life?

How might Jesus be calling you to trust His timing or participate in a miracle He wants to perform in your life?

A Prayer Opportunity

If you have been resurrected from spiritual death to spiritual life, prayerfully consider: Are you still walking around bound in your grave clothes? Why not begin confessing whatever binds you and put on the righteous garments of praise?

Day Five

Passion or Profession?

John 12:1–8

Father, as we bow before Your holy throne today, we cannot help but rejoice! Thank You for Your goodness, for Your kindness, for the way You walk before us and behind us. You are the Provider of our soul! We love You! Amen.

My husband asked for my measurements last night. I was horrified and curious at the same time. Then I noticed the Cabella's catalogue in his hand. In planning for a fly fishing trip, he needed my measurements so he could order some waders for me. After he teasingly insulted me by guessing them, he asked for a tape measure. Slowly I handed him the tape measure, then thought better. I decided to measure myself! That way I could hold the tape measure loosely where I wanted to and hold it tightly in other areas!

The tape measure is a glaring reminder of our physical stature. In the same way, the Bible is a reminder of our spiritual stature. We do not necessarily like for our lives to be measured by either! We may want to hold some Scriptures closely to us and others loosely!

Measurements are important because they tell us how we are doing. Physically, measurements tell us how we are weighing in. Physicians tell us to measure our bodies. If our waist is larger than it should be, we may be prone to certain diseases.

Nutritionists tell us to measure our portions of food. If we overeat or undereat we will become unhealthy.

Spiritually, God tells us to measure! Do we have Christ's Spirit in us? Are we walking by the flesh or by the Spirit? Are we doing good works that cause others to glorify our Father who is in heaven? Are we fulfilling our roles as Christ's ambassadors and telling others about Jesus?

In today's study we will find Jesus measuring people's hearts, professions, and actions. **Read John 11:45–57.**

As you recall, things are coming to a climax in Jerusalem. Jesus' miracle of resurrecting Lazarus from the dead has caused the Pharisees to be more determined than ever to kill Him. **Why was there no denying that Jesus had brought Lazarus back from the dead?**

At this point people's hearts were measured! There was no honesty in denying that Jesus had the power of God, to give life, to raise the dead!

Principle:
God measures people's hearts.

How did the following people's hearts measure up?

John 11:45—The hearts of many of the Jews

John 11:46—The hearts of other Jews

John 11:47–48—The hearts of the chief priests and Pharisees

John 11:49–53—The heart of Caiaphas, the high priest

This cannot help but make us sad. The high priest was to represent the people to God and God to the people. Instead, the high priest was plotting to kill God!

Oh, may we be ever so careful as God's priests to not do anything to deny God in our life. The term *grieve* is used to describe what we do to God when we sin, when we do not let

God take His rightful place in our hearts, homes, finances, marriage, business. We "grieve" or "quench" the Holy Spirit who abides in us! What a strong warning for us as we see the religious leaders quenching and grieving Jesus!

Principle:
**If Jesus is who He says He is,
then I should give Him His rightful place in my life!**

Jesus, no longer able to walk publicly, left Bethany and went to Ephraim, where He stayed until six days before the Passover. **Read John 12:1–8,** where we pick back up with Martha. Friends and family were all in place. We know several of them fairly well by now.

What were the following people doing?

Martha

Lazarus

Mary

How nice it must have been for Jesus to be with them. Each one in this home had been changed by the Master's touch. Martha was no longer looking around to see what others were doing. Lazarus' heart was ticking away. **Where was Mary?**

When Taylor and Lauren were little they enjoyed a book called *Where's Waldo?* Each page was filled with pictures of animals, people, vehicles, and outdoor and indoor scenes. What made the book fun for children (and parents) was to search through the many faces in the crowd and find Waldo in his predictable red shirt. "There he is!" whoever found him would exclaim.

I cannot help but think our heavenly Father smiled when He looked from heaven amidst all the crowds and faces and asked, "Where's Mary?"

Where's Mary?
Luke 10:39

Where's Mary?
John 11:32

Where's Mary?
John 12:3

Who did the people follow?
John 11:20, 31

Whose name is recorded that the Jews went to, who believed in Jesus?
John 11:45

Principle:
People follow passion, not just profession.

People want to see, not just hear, our profession of faith.

Are you passionate for Christ? People want to see, not just hear, our profession of faith. People need to see. Jesus explained that we are to be the light of the world as a city set on a hill. People in darkness are drawn to light. Be the light of Jesus! Why? Jesus tells us to let our light shine so people can see our good works and glorify our Father in heaven (Matthew 5:16).

How? Follow Mary's example. Begin and end your day at Jesus' feet! And in between, go to Him as often as you can. Develop intimacy with your Savior. Plant yourself in the soil of God's Word. Abide in Christ. Be rooted in prayer, and you will grow into His likeness. People will begin to identify you as having been with Jesus (Acts 4:13)!

Reread John 12:2. Martha is serving as before, but tonight she is not looking to see what Mary is doing. The heart of

Martha is measured and found peaceful.

Read John 12:3–8. Then the heart of Mary was measured. In John 12:3, the following words are emphasized in Greek: *very costly*, *pure*, and *with her hair*.

A pound was equal to 12 ounces. *Nard* was an expensive perfume, an anointing oil made from an herb from northern India. **How much was the perfume worth? John 12:5**

Three hundred *denarii* was approximately what a rural worker would earn in eleven to twelve months! Can you imagine the look in the eyes of the observers as Mary extravagantly anointed Jesus with her love?

Did Lazarus tell her to stop?

Did Martha complain?

The hearts of the disciples were measured. The heart of Judas was measured.

Consider the scene. It is one of Jesus' last nights. Jesus has been welcomed into the home of Simon the leper. Martha is serving. The disciples are gathered. Mary quietly moves closer and closer to her Lord. The room is hushed as they watch her take a pound of very costly perfume and pour it over Jesus. They watch as she loosens her hair. They look to see if Jesus objects. He does not.

The home immediately fills with the fragrance of the perfume lavished upon Jesus' feet. The perfume runs and drips on Jesus' feet. Mary wipes Jesus' dusty, tired feet with her hair.

Where's Mary?

The room is quiet as Jesus looks upon this child of God who has truly listened to Him and understands who He is and that He is about to die. We see Mary's passion. As Mary pours out all that she is and has on Jesus, as she lavishes Him with her love, Judas pours out all that he is and has on Jesus. The heart of Judas is measured.

What does Judas follow Mary's action with? John 12:4–6

Words! Judas' words sound so noble, so caring! Judas, by the profession of his mouth, cares about the poor, cares about the people. **Did the profession of Judas' mouth measure up to his true profession—a thief?**
❏ Yes
❏ No

Read John 12:7–8. What does Jesus say in response to Judas?

Let Mary alone, Martha. Let Mary alone, Judas.

One of the things that hurts my heart regarding the body of Christ is when believers are critical of how other believers express their love and worship of God. Are you a Judas? Would Jesus ever want to say to you, "Leave her alone! She is truly worshipping Me. You are focused on her, not Me at all! You profess adoration, but I measure your heart by your words and actions. You are a thief. You steal joy. You steal passion. You pilfer what is put into God's treasury by your critical spirit and tongue."

How does your heart measure up?

Where was Mary? Mary was worshipping at Jesus' feet. Where are we in relation to God? Who are our eyes focused on? Ourselves? Others? Jesus? Are we a worshipper of Jesus or a professor of Jesus or both?

What do we miss by not sitting at Jesus feet?

What opportunities for worship and service come and go?

What worldly possessions, time, or energy do we cling to when the wisest investment of our time is to worship at Jesus' feet?

Christ measured Mary's heart and Judas' heart. How are they remembered?

Mary will be known forever for her fragrant love and intimacy with the Savior. Judas will be remembered for his stench and betrayal of Jesus.

Principle:
Our actions are measured in light of eternity. Extravagant love for Jesus is seen in a life poured out for Him.

Apply God's Word

Mary poured out her love, then carried the fragrance of her intimacy with Jesus about the home. The fragrance of our life is an indicator of our intimacy, or lack of it, with Jesus. **How does Mary's extravagant love challenge you?**

The priests did not acknowledge Jesus as Lord. **How does a believer "quench the Spirit" today?**

Up Close and Personal

How do you measure in terms of taking care of your heart:

Physically?
Spiritually?

What fragrance do you wear as you move about your home, grocery store, and work? The fragrance of busyness, self-centeredness, disgruntlement, worldliness, or having been with Christ?

What works are you doing that cause people to glorify your heavenly Father? If you have none, what must happen for you to fulfill your destiny as a Christian to do so?

How do you model to others being at Jesus' feet?

When the religious leaders denied Jesus' power and sought to "quench" Him, the Scripture says Jesus was no longer able to walk about. The Spirit does not ever leave the believer. However, Jesus can be quenched from moving powerfully in a believer's life when one denies Jesus as Lord.

How free is Jesus to move in your life? How might you have grieved or denied Him as Lord of your life?

A Prayer Opportunity

Mary poured out her love in extravagant worship. Today we can confess our sin and pour out our adoration and worship of God through praise, prayers, and our lives. Sit at Jesus' feet now. Pour out what is on your heart and mind.

Week Five
Thinking It Over

Please look back over your lesson and prayerfully complete the following.

1. What was most meaningful to you in your study of Martha and Mary from:

Day 1

Day 2

Day 3

Day 4

Day 5

2. How did God speak to your heart as you studied Martha's life?

3. In what way does this lesson stimulate you to move beyond being a woman who only professes her faith to being a woman of passion?

4. How is God challenging you to keep your heart healthy?

Physically:

Spiritually:

5. What "golden nugget" of truth do you want to remember from this week?

6. What verse do you want to remember from this week's lesson?

7. What is the prayerful cry of your heart in relation to this week's study?

Week Six

He Saw the Pure Me

Day One

Mary Magdalene
Matthew 27:56, 61; 28:1; Mark 15:40–41; 16:1–19; Luke 8:1–2, 24:10; John 19:25, 20:1–18

An amazing reality is the love of Jesus Christ for us. No matter what our situation, God sees the pure person He created us to be.

A significant health concern today is the toxins we take into our bodies through the foods we eat and the air we breathe. Dr. Don Colbert, in his book *Toxic Relief*, warns, "While you are going about your daily business, a war is raging inside your body at the molecular level. Free radicals are machine-gunning microscopic shrapnel, injuring your cells throughout the day."

What toxins do we need to guard against that stimulate free radicals which can set the stage for cancer, heart disease, and numerous other diseases? Many food additives, fried foods, polyunsaturated fats, pesticides, industrial chemicals, radiation,

cigarette smoke, and air pollution contribute to disease.

Toxins ⇨ Damaged Cells ⇨ Disease

As toxins are to the body, so evil is to our soul. The toxins of spiritual life are complacency, fast food sermons, preservative liturgy, depleted spiritual soil, chemically infused relationships, and pride-saturated egos; these turn spirit-filled Christians into worldly Christians.

The principle we will look at this week is that God has given us everything we need for life. For our physical life, He has given us water, plants, grains, fishes, and meats. For our spiritual life, He has given us forgiveness of sin, redemption, and abundant life through Jesus Christ our Lord.

God cares about our body, for with our body we live as His temple, acting as His ambassador in the world, carrying His light to the world.

God cares about our spirit, for it is with our spirit we commune and fellowship with God, receive the blessing of His presence, and bear the fullness and fruit of His Spirit. God cares about our body and spirit, and has therefore provided everything we need for life. May we stand against assaults on both the physical and spiritual fronts!

Mary Magdalene knew firsthand what it was like to be held in the grip of demons. Her deliverance and changed life are proof that it is never too late to change.

God had plans for Mary Magdalene, and His plans included more than her cleansing. His plans included her knowing abundant life.

God has plans for you and me. His plans include more than our being free of toxins and the influence of evil. God's plans include our being part of His work and knowing abundant life.

In today's study we will answer the following questions:
1. What toxins do I need to guard against in my body and spirit?
2. What three changes characterize a person who is a part of the kingdom of God?
3. What two choices can I make today to invest in Jesus as He has invested in me?
4. How is Jesus' passion for mankind evident?
5. What important last words did Jesus speak before His ascension?

Mary Magdalene is a remarkable woman. She holds a place in the hallmark of women in the Bible as being the first to see our risen Lord! What did she do that brought such honor and privilege? Why was she the first person in all of eternity to proclaim the good news, "He is risen!" even as the angels were the first to proclaim, "He is born!"

Unlike Mary the mother of Jesus and Mary of Bethany, we know nothing about the family life of Mary Magdalene. We have no idea how she was raised, nor if she ever married, had children, or family. However, there are several facts about Mary that we do know. **Read Luke 8:1–3. Where was Mary from?**

Magdala means "tower" or "castle." In the time of Christ, Magdala was a thriving, populous town on the coast of Galilee about three miles from Capernaum, known for its dye works and textile factories. **How did Mary's life change after she met Jesus? What was she doing?**

Magdala was a small town between Capernaum and Tiberius in Galilee.

Who did Mary travel with?

Imagine both the joy and the challenges of traveling with a group of such varied personalities and backgrounds! Mary's life would have been far from calm! Women traveling and supporting Jesus and the disciples out of their own means would have been viewed as scandalous in that day. However, like the forgiven woman in Luke 7:36–50, Mary Magdalene, delivered from much, loved and served Jesus with all she had. **Whose kingdom and power had Mary been living under prior to meeting Jesus?**

Mary Magdalene had lived under the kingdom of Satan, evil, and demons! It is easy to quickly read over Mary's life prior to her coming to Jesus. However, if we ponder what it would have been like to be possessed by seven demons, we rejoice even more at her deliverance into God's kingdom!

The reality of demons is taught throughout the Bible. Ponder what the word *demon, daimonion* means: "a deity; a super-

natural spirit of a bad nature, devil."

Demons are evil spirits, messengers and ministers of the devil. They are referred to in all the Gospels as well as Acts, 1 Corinthians, 1 Timothy, James, and Revelation. Jesus, as well as His disciples, cast them out. Mary had been possessed, in the power of seven demons.

Look up the following Scriptures about demons. As you do, ponder and record what it must have been like for Mary Magdalene to be possessed by seven demons.

Luke 8:27–29

Mark 5:5

Seven evil spirits had held fast to Mary's body, spirit, and mind. Jesus freed Mary of demon possession and evil! Praise the Lord!

Who would you follow if you were Mary Magdalene?
❏ Jesus
❏ Satan
❏ World

Who would you contribute to if you were Mary Magdalene?
❏ Jesus
❏ Satan
❏ World

Who are we following, for is it not by the grace of God we are saved? Who are we giving to, for is it not by the grace of God we will spend eternity in heaven? Satan, the ruler of demons, is not able to possess the believer, but he can still have subtle and devastating effects on believers' lives if we do not stand against him. **Record how Satan can influence believers based on the following Scriptures. See the example for the first Scripture below.**

Matthew 16:21–23—To set my mind on my interests, not God's

Matthew 16:24

Luke 22:31–34

Ephesians 4:26–27

Ephesians 5:15–16

Ephesians 5:17

Ephesians 6:10–14

Ephesians 6:18

As we look at God's deliverance of Mary, may we be mindful of the weapons of our warfare that God has given the believer to stand against Satan!

Apply God's Word
What part of the definition of demon struck you as odd or was new to you?

Which of the Scriptures that spoke of our stand against Satan was applicable and a good warning to be heeded by you?

Up Close and Personal
Satan was defeated at the cross, but remains the prince of the power of the air, on the loose. Christians are citizens of heaven, living as ambassadors on earth, where Satan continues his guerrilla warfare. That is why the Bible tells the believer to put on the full armor of God. Earth is the battleground. You are the building, the temple of God, the one the fiery darts of the evil one are aimed for. If Satan cannot have you, he will attempt to destroy your health, your witness, your walking in the good works God prepared for you, and

your effectiveness in God's kingdom.

What do you understand your role to be in the Kingdom of God on earth, where Satan rules as the prince of the world?

What is your understanding of your need to be prayerful and armored against the schemes and influences of Satan?

Have you ever been as Peter, and not believed Satan could touch you or tempt you? Did you believe you would not yield or give in, and then you did?

What difference does it make to you to know that Satan is real and his demons do his bidding in the world?

Although no one but Jesus Christ lived a wholly pure life, Christians can be increasingly sensitive to the amount of toxins we allow in our body and spirit. The following are toxic to our body and spirit in excess. **Which are you tempted with?**

Physically:
❑ Foods with preservatives
❑ Alcohol abuse
❑ Foods with additives
❑ Fast foods
❑ Fried foods
❑ Cigarettes
❑ Polyunsaturated and trans fats
❑ Greasy hamburgers
❑ Saturated fats
❑ Excessive amounts of refined sugars
❑ Other

Spiritually:
❑ Pride
❑ Envy
❑ Anger
❑ Impatience

- ❏ Lack of self control
- ❏ Covetousness
- ❏ Lust
- ❏ Slothfulness
- ❏ Other

A Prayer Opportunity

To deny the effects of toxins in our body is to deny warnings given to us by health care professionals and nutritionists. To deny the existence and influence of Satan and the toxic effects of sin for us spiritually is to deny our Lord's warnings. Prayerfully consider if you have been negligent and not paid attention to the warnings given to you both physically and spiritually. Record the cry of your heart to God.

Day Two

Delivered Into God's Kingdom

Matthew 12:46–50

Heavenly Father, as we approach the study of Your Word today, may we be mindful of the goodness and blessings that are ours in Christ Jesus. Awaken us to the inheritance we received when You delivered us out of the kingdom of darkness and into Your glorious Light! In Jesus' name, Amen.

I will never forget when American soldiers rescued Private Jessica Lynch from Iraq. Television stations carried the good news, as the eyes of the nation celebrated the rescue of one American daughter from enemy ground.

Turn to the heavens. Picture the same scene. One daughter, captured by the prince of the world, is held captive by demons. She has no way to free herself. Then, Jesus came to her. Think of the celebration in heaven when God's daughter, Mary Magdalene, was rescued from the grip of Satan and delivered into God's kingdom! If we think the face of Jessica Lynch was known in America, we cannot imagine the face of Mary Magdalene streaming across the heavens!

Read the following passages in which Jesus, by way of

parables, tells us what happens in heaven when one person, such as Mary Magdalene, is delivered from the kingdom of darkness. Record the key word(s) that describe the emotion and reaction in heaven.

Luke 15:1–7
verses 6–7

Luke 15:8–10
verses 9–10

Principle:
There is joy in heaven over one sinner who repents, over one person Jesus delivers from bondage!

Mary Magdalene's life was different not only because of what she was released from, but also because of what she was released to. Mary Magdalene was delivered out of the kingdom of darkness and transferred into the kingdom of light! What did her deliverance mean to her?
• A change of direction
• A change of citizenship
• A change of family

A Change of Direction
Mary was headed in one direction when she met Jesus. Her spirit was possessed by demons. **Read Matthew 13:47–50.**
Had Mary Magdalene's soul not been delivered, where would she have been headed?

A Change of Citizenship
Citizenship in the time of Jesus meant everything, just as it does today. If you were a Roman citizen, you were afforded certain rights and protection that non-citizens did not have. Mindful of the protection and privilege citizenship meant, Paul wrote about the believer's citizenship.
   Read and record what Paul explained regarding a Christian's citizenship. Philippians 3:20

Because Christians are citizens of heaven, what will Jesus do one day so that we are able to live with Him for eternity? Philippians 3:21

Read Ephesians 2:1–3. Before a person becomes a citizen of heaven, how is that person described? Check all that are true.
❏ Dead in our trespasses and sins
❏ Walking according to the course of this world
❏ Walking according to the prince of the power of the air
❏ Walking according to the spirit that is working in the sons of disobedience
❏ Living in the lusts of our flesh
❏ Indulging the desires of the flesh and mind
❏ By nature, children of wrath.

All who call on the name of the Lord will be saved!

What was required for one to be able to be a citizen of heaven? Check all that apply based on Ephesians 2:4–9
❏ God being rich in mercy
❏ God loving us, even when we were dead in our transgressions
❏ God making us alive together with Christ
❏ God saving us by grace
❏ God raising us and seating us with Christ Jesus in the heavenly places
❏ God being kind toward us in Christ Jesus.
❏ God giving us the gift of salvation.

No wonder Paul poured from his heart, "Oh, the depth of the riches both of the wisdom and knowledge of God! How unsearchable are His judgments and unfathomable His ways!" (Romans 11:33).

Principle:
Christians are citizens of heaven because of God's great mercy, love, grace, and kindness.

The blessings of our citizenship will be known in full when we

are ushered into the gates of heaven and see our Lord high and lifted up! Oh, that will be a reunion! We will fall at Christ's feet and cry, "Holy, Holy, Holy!"

Mary Magdalene's citizenship was transferred from the kingdom of Satan to the kingdom of God. She realized it and stayed close to her Savior. She contributed to His needs and served Him. Do we?

A Change of Family

The believer is no longer a citizen of the world, over which Satan reigns as prince of the power of the air. Our citizenship is transferred to heaven, to the Kingdom of God. God paid for our citizenship with the blood of the Lamb, His Son.

But that is not all! Christians are more than citizens of heaven. Christians are part of God's family! **What did Jesus say that would have made Mary Magdalene's heart soar? Matthew 12:46–50**

Imagine being Mary Magdalene. She has been under the prince of darkness, possessed by demons. Now Jesus, the Son of God, heaven sent, calls *her* His sister, His mother. No wonder she worshipped the ground Jesus walked on. No wonder we will find her at the cross and at the tomb. No wonder she was the first human being to see the resurrected Lord Jesus!

Oh, that we might grasp the depth and richness of Jesus' grace. Does Jesus mention Mary's past? Does He remind her of where she has come from? Does Jesus say she cannot serve because of what she was involved in prior to coming to Him? No. No. No.

Dear friends, how can we be under bondage from our past if we are Christians? Do you realize that is an oxymoron? It is a contradiction of who you are! If you are a Christian you are *not* under bondage. **Record John 8:36, which describes our freedom from the bondage of sin.**

Christians, as members of God's family, are not only free from the penalty of sin, which is death; we are free from bondage to sin. Jesus and Mary Magdalene did not live in relation to her past, but her present and future. If you suffer from recurring

God paid for our citizenship with the blood of the Lamb, His Son.

thoughts or stirrings of guilt over your past, remember Mary Magdalene. **Memorize John 8:36.**

As a family member, you have a right to the following claims; know them and stand firm in them.

Regarding your past sin:
- Jesus forgives you. Luke 11:4
- Jesus has taken away your sin. John 1:29
- Jesus has washed away your sins. Acts 22:16
- Jesus has already died for your sins. 1 Corinthians 15:3 (You don't need to die any more for them. Once is enough, and Jesus has already died.)

For present sin:
- Confess your sin to God. 1 John 1:9
- Go and sin no more. John 8:11
- Read the Bible to help you not sin. 1 John 2:1
- Walk by the Spirit so you do not carry out the lust of the flesh. Galatians 5:16
- Confess your sin to a strong Christian, and ask them to pray for you. James 5:16

Imagine! We are a part of God's family!

Principle:
God has adopted the redeemed
into His kingdom family.

Apply God's Word

Mary Magdalene was delivered out of the kingdom of darkness and into the kingdom of heaven, to the praise and glory of God! It meant a change of direction, a change of citizenship, and a change of family. If you are a Christian, you have been delivered out of darkness and into the kingdom of heaven.

Which verse or teaching from today was most meaningful to you and why?

What does it mean to you that you have been transferred out of the kingdom of darkness and into God's glorious light?

Imagine! We are a part of God's family!

Up Close and Personal

Toxic thoughts can affect our mind and health even as toxic foods can affect our body.

What toxic thoughts do you need to refuse, based on your being rescued from the domain of darkness and being transferred into God's glorious light?

Which of the truths regarding past and present sin do you need to digest?

A Prayer Opportunity

Let the cry of your heart go before the Lord in prayer and praise.

Day Three
Mary Chose Jesus' Presence and Purpose
Luke 8:4–21; 12:22–51

Father, thank You for Your Word, which enlightens us. Thank You for Jesus' presence, which comforts us. Thank You for Jesus' light, which guides us. May our heart's desire be to walk by Your Word, live in Your presence, and follow Christ's light every day of our life. Amen.

On my first scuba diving adventure, I was totally afraid! My only training was a quick lesson at a resort pool. As I sat and listened to every word the scuba instructor said, I became

increasingly unsure of myself. I made a quick decision that my best course of action would be to stay as close to the instructor as possible. That way, if I got in trouble, I would be near help. With a prayer and a weak smile to my husband, Keith, who had always dreamed of us scuba diving together, I plodded (yes, you can plod even with flippers on) into the deep blue ocean until I could no longer stand. Then I quickly submerged and followed my instructor. Where he went, I went. Every time he turned to check on the others, who were off exploring, I was close by his side, mask-to-mask, eyeball-to-eyeball. I could count his eyelashes!

I wonder if that is how Mary Magdalene felt! If I had been possessed by seven demons, guess whose side I would want to be by? I would want to stay close enough to Jesus to count His eyelashes! Over the last two days we have looked at how Mary Magdalene was delivered from the kingdom of darkness into the kingdom of light.

Today, we are going to see two tangible ways Mary chose to invest her life in Jesus. We are going to discover that Mary chose to invest her time in Jesus' presence. We are also going to see that Mary chose to invest her life in Jesus' purposes. Does everyone touched by Jesus respond as Mary Magdalene did? No, unfortunately. Out of the ten lepers Jesus healed, only one came back to even thank Him. May we be like Mary, and not the nine unthankful lepers.

Mary Chose Jesus' Presence

Mary chose to invest her time and being in Jesus' presence. She had lived under the dominion of darkness. Now she desired to learn what it meant to live under the dominion of God. Rather than return to Magdala, to her old practices, friends, habits, and temptations, Mary chose to live in Christ's presence. Are we that wise?

Mary chose Christ's presence, listened to His teachings, and gave to Him out of the abundance of her love. She was cleansed. Now she was ready to be filled. How could Mary be filled, possessed, and held by the Spirit of God? How could her mind be under His influence? Mary could:

- Listen to Jesus' words when He taught the crowds.
- Linger over Jesus' words, meditating on them after the crowds left.
- Learn to walk as a child of the kingdom of God, following

Jesus' example.

What blessings Mary Magdalene received living in Christ's presence! Jesus' teachings are familiar to many of us. But what if you had never heard them? What if you were coming out of demon possession, or a bad marriage, or had just left a child in jail, or worse, one to death? What if you had just been laid off from your job? What if you were widowed and afraid? What if a major conflict erupted between you and a close friend or associate?

Following are some of the teachings Mary would have heard as she invested her life in Jesus and abided in His presence. **Look up the following Scriptures and record Jesus' teaching. Then record what that teaching might have meant to Mary as she was learning to walk as a child of the Light.**

Luke 12:22

  Jesus said:

  What it would have meant to Mary:

Luke 12:24

  Jesus said:

  What it would have meant to Mary:

Luke 12:32

  Jesus said:

  What it would have meant to Mary:

Luke 12:33–34

  Jesus said:

  What it would have meant to Mary:

Luke 12:40–44

Jesus said:

What it would have meant to Mary:

Luke 12:51

Jesus said:

What it would have meant to Mary:

Principle:
Mary learned about kingdom life
by investing her time in the King's presence.

Where Jesus went, Mary went. No doubt, there were times of comfort and times of discomfort, times of inconvenience and times when things went smoothly. There were times when they were welcomed and times when they were not. In each situation, Mary learned how to walk with Christ.

Mary Chose Jesus' Purposes as Her Own
Luke 8:2–3 tells us Mary Magdalene chose to invest her life in Jesus. She chose not only to invest her life in His presence; she chose Jesus' life purposes as her own. She joined Jesus in His work of spreading the good news of the kingdom of God.

Jesus' ministry required funding, and while Jesus and the disciples spoke, taught, and healed, Mary gave financially. Although she could have returned to her past life, she did not.

She could have yielded to demonic temptations, to sorcery. She did not. She could have become complacent, forgetting what the Savior had done for her. She did not. She could have taken Jesus for granted, as many do today. She did not. Rather than Mary distancing herself from Jesus as she grew in her faith, Mary grew closer to Jesus and helped others in their faith walk.

Have we invested our lives in Jesus, as He has invested His life in ours?

Apply God's Word

Mary's deliverance from the kingdom of Satan was her entrance into the kingdom of God. Mary chose to invest her life in Jesus' presence, learning what it meant to be a child of the kingdom of God. Mary chose to invest her life in Jesus' purpose—to seek and to save the lost, to proclaim the good news of the kingdom of God. **To what degree have you invested your life in the presence and purposes of Jesus?**

To what degree are you learning and practicing Jesus' teachings and walking in His light?

Following are the kingdom teachings that we looked up in relation to Mary's life. Now let us contemplate them in light of our lives. **For each of Jesus' teachings listed below, consider what Jesus is saying to you. Be specific as you relate Jesus' kingdom teachings to your life.**

Luke 12:22—Jesus said not to worry about life.
What Jesus is saying to me is:

Luke 12:23—Jesus said life is more than food.
What Jesus is saying to me is:

Luke 12:24—Jesus said your life is valuable to God.
What Jesus is saying to me is:

Luke 12:25—Jesus said worry cannot add a single hour to life.
What Jesus is saying to me is:

Luke 12:31—Jesus said to seek God's kingdom.

What Jesus is saying to me is:

Luke 12:32—Jesus said not to be afraid, the Father has gladly chosen to give you the kingdom of heaven.
What Jesus is saying to me is:

Luke 12:33–34—Jesus said to invest your treasure and heart in heaven.
What Jesus is saying to me is:

Luke 12:40–44—Jesus said to be faithful, ready, on the alert for His return.
What Jesus is saying to me is:

Luke 12:51—Jesus said that He did not come to bring peace, but division.
What Jesus is saying to me is:

Up Close and Personal

What most challenges you about Mary Magdalene investing her life in Jesus' presence and teachings?

What most challenges you about Mary Magdalene investing her life in Jesus' purposes?

Mary learned about kingdom living and was blessed. Which teaching of kingdom living has blessed you?

How are you investing your life in Jesus' purposes? If you

are not, how might Jesus be drawing you to join Him?

A Prayer Opportunity

What has God prompted you to think about in relation to your own life? Whatever it is, pray about it now. Express your love and adoration to God, as well as any confession for not staying as close to Jesus through prayer, Bible study, meditation, and/or service as you might have. Ask Jesus to help you live more by His kingdom teachings. Ask God to show you how you can join Him in His proclamation of the kingdom of God.

Day Four

Mary Magdalene Shared Jesus' Passion

John 11:47–57; 12:8–43, Luke 23:27–34

Lord, as we approach Your Word today, may we take it to heart! May we learn from Mary's example how to remain in Your presence and share Your passion. In Jesus' name, Amen.

"Blackout 2003" was the largest power outage in North America's history. In nine seconds, 61,800 megawatts were lost and 50 million people from the Atlantic to the Great Lakes and south to Ohio were abruptly left without power. People were shocked and left in darkness.

Some 2000 years earlier, there was another blackout, like none other in history. The Light of the World died. The good news of the cross is that the Light may have gone out for three days, but the power of the Holy One was stronger than any force of darkness or death!

The Passover, which Mary Magdalene and the Jews were preparing to celebrate, commemorated the deliverance of the Jews from Egyptian bondage by Moses. The Passover celebrated the night the angel of death passed over the homes of the Jews who had placed the blood of the lamb over their

doorway. The Jews waited for the promised Messiah, who would once again bring deliverance to the Jews. News of Jesus had spread.

Some wondered if Jesus might be the promised Messiah. **Read John 11:55. What was happening as the Passover approached?**

Read John 11:56. Who were the Jews seeking?

What were they wondering?

Read John 11:47–54, 57. Why was there such anticipation in the air? Why did people question if Jesus would even come to the Passover?

What terrible news did Jesus confirm to the disciples and those gathered six days before the Passover? John 12:7–8

What added to the excitement and tension in the air? John 12:9–11

The excitement of Jesus being recognized as the Messiah climaxed the next day. **Read John 12:12–15. What happened?**

Imagine Mary Magdalene watching all of this. Imagine her elation as well as her being perplexed at Jesus' words about His death. Imagine her quandary as she watched Jesus sit upon the colt and ride into the lion's den of those seeking to kill Him. **Read John 12:17.**

What did people who had seen Jesus raise Lazarus from the dead continue to do?
❏ Not believe
❏ Testify about Jesus

Read John 12:18–21. The Jews were not the only ones wanting to see Jesus. Who else sought Him?
❑ The world
❑ Greeks

The Pharisees did not realize the truth of their statements about Jesus. **Record the two statements the Pharisees made which were fulfillments of prophecy.**

John 11:49–50

John 12:19

The next few verses in John 12:23–32 would have had a profound impact on Mary Magdalene. **What would she have heard, being in the crowd that day?**

Jesus saying:

A voice out of heaven saying:

What would have impacted her even more, considering her experience with the ruler of this world? John 12:30–32

Mary must have been in tears at this point. The crowd's question was a good one. **What were they wondering? John 12:34**
❑ If Christ was eternal, how could He die?
❑ What did Jesus mean by "lifted up"?

The crowd could not understand how or why the Christ would be lifted up to die since the Law said that the Christ would be eternal.

What reaction of the crowd did Mary Magdalene observe? Check all that are true. John 12:37, 42
❑ Many did not believe in Jesus.
❑ Even many of the rulers believed in Jesus.

What would have broken Mary Magdalene's heart as she observed the crowds and the faces and hearts of the rulers? John 12:43

At this time, we get a further look into the heart of our precious Savior. **What beautiful words are spoken about Jesus' love? John 13:1**

Jesus loved His own to the end. Jesus warned His followers He was going to die. **What impact would Jesus' words in John 13:33 have had on Mary Magdalene?**

Mary, who had chosen to stay in Jesus' presence, now chooses to share His passion. The grief of the impending separation is all too real. Jesus is not hiding His imminent death from His followers. The religious leaders are not hiding their desire to kill Jesus. As the Passover moves ahead, the sacrificial Lamb is moved to the forefront by the Jews where He will be slain by the priests for the atonement of the sins of the world.

At sunset, Jesus celebrates the Passover with His disciples, ordains the Lord's Supper, agonizes in Gethsemane, is betrayed by Judas with a kiss, and is taken before Annas, then Caiaphas at dawn.

Jesus is brought before Pilate for the sentence of crucifixion. Pilate announces he finds no guilt in Jesus, then has Jesus flogged with a leather whip that had pieces of bone or metal imbedded in its thongs, a cruel punishment used by the Romans only on murderers and traitors, and from which many died. With the Roman cohort gathered around Jesus they stripped Him and put a scarlet robe on His bloody back. They put a crown of thorns on our Savior's head. They put a reed in His right hand and knelt down before our Lord and mocked Him, saying, "Hail, King of the Jews!" They spit on Jesus and took the reed from His hand and beat Him on the head. They took the scarlet robe off Jesus and put His own garments back on His beaten, bleeding body. They laid the heavy wooden beam across Jesus' flogged shoulders.

The crowd had stood and roared, "Crucify Him!" and Mary Magdalene had stood with the others, in horror and

Jesus loved His own to the end.

shock. With tears flowing and no doubt revulsion in her stomach for the horrors inflicted on her Lord, she watched as Jesus carried the weight of our cross up the hill to Golgotha. **Read Luke 23:27–31. In all of Jesus' pain and suffering, to whom did Jesus turn and speak?**

May we never forget to stand by the cross when we are tempted to not forgive!

Mary Magdalene, in the crowd, would have heard Jesus' words. As the nails were pounded into His flesh and Jesus was lifted up on the cross in agonizing pain, could she believe what she heard through the sneers of the rulers and the mocking of the soldiers? How did Mary hear Jesus? She stood by the cross of Jesus. **Who stood by the cross with her? John 19:25**

As the soldiers mocked and the rulers and other people sneered, the women and John stood at the cross of Jesus, watching as Jesus' life ebbed away. **Clinging to Jesus' every breath, what words did they hear Jesus pray? Luke 23:34**

Oh, the divine example God the Father gives us in Jesus! May we never forget to stand by the cross when we are tempted not to forgive! **As insults were hurled at Jesus, "Save yourself," what was Jesus doing? Luke 23:36–43**
❑ **Saving one more sinner.**
❑ **Saving Himself.**

Oh, the love that drew salvation's plan, the love that brought it down to man. Jesus hung on the cross doing what He had come into the world to do, up to His last breath.

Jesus saw who was standing by the cross. Are we standing by the cross today? Or is the cross too uncomfortable or too much of an embarrassment for us to stand by? Are we afraid, like the disciples who fled when the Romans came to arrest Jesus? Are we well intentioned as Peter, but in reality "peter out" when called to stand up for our faith?

Jesus saw who was at the cross. I pray He sees me by the cross when He looks. I pray He sees you.

Those were the last words Mary heard before darkness fell

upon the land as the Light of the World's life ebbed away. Then, Jesus' voice pierced the darkness with words that must have pierced the hearts of those who loved Him. **Read Matthew 27:46–47. Record Jesus' words from the cross.**

Are we standing by the cross today?

How could the Heavenly Father allow His only begotten Son to hang forsaken on the cross? John 3:16 answers that question! Forsaken of God, a curse on the cross, Jesus knew everything was accomplished and asked for a drink, saying, "I am thirsty" (John 19:28). Then Jesus cried with a loud voice, "It is finished!" It is brought to a close! The salvation of mankind is accomplished! The Lamb had been sacrificed for the sins of all nations.

Principle:
Jesus did what He came to do. He sought and saved those who are lost. Jesus offered Himself a living and holy sacrifice, acceptable unto God as an atonement for man's sin.

Following Jesus' cry that the price had been paid for man's redemption, He cried out His final words. **Record Jesus' final words. Luke 23:46**

Jesus' final words were, "Father, into Your hands I commit My spirit." The earth stood silent as the Light of the World went out. Jesus breathed His last.

"No!" must have been the cry as the women who loved Jesus watched Him yield up His Spirit to God.

Father, how You sent Your Son, we'll never understand. Lord Jesus, how You hung on the cross, we'll never comprehend. Help us now, in this hour, to not forget Your love, but to take Your message, proclaim Your Kingdom, and bring glory to You above.

Apply God's Word

Think back over the events of the cross. What is most moving regarding what Jesus did for you?

Which of Jesus' words from the cross most touched you and why?

Up Close and Personal

Jesus' passion for you is evident. Are you passionate for Him?

How is your passion for Jesus evident?

Prayerfully consider where you stand in relation to Jesus and the cross.
❏ I forget the price and suffering Jesus paid for my sins to be forgiven.
❏ I live in wonder and awe of my Savior, thanking Him for dying for me.
❏ I have moved away from the cross, but I want to move closer to Jesus.
❏ I want to know Jesus more intimately and serve His purposes more faithfully.

A Prayer Opportunity

Any time we have an opportunity to pray, we should take it. Now is one such time. Confess any resistance to the cross you have had, realizing that it is only by Jesus' death you are saved. If you are not sure you are a Christian and you want to be, pray now. *Dear Jesus, I know I am a sinner. I know I have done wrong things, and that apart from Your forgiveness, I will die in my sins. Please forgive me. Please wash away all my sins, and let me come to You in heaven and live with You forever. In Jesus' name, Amen.* If you are a Christian, what prayer is on your heart?

Day Five

He Is Risen

Matthew 27:57–66, John 20:1–18

Heavenly Father, thank You for the gift of life You give us in Your Son! May we be instruments of Your righteousness and proclaim with Mary Magdalene the good news, "Jesus is risen!" In His name we pray, Amen.

After the darkest day, the darkest night followed. After Jesus committed His Spirit into His Father's hands, a soldier pierced Jesus' side. Blood and water flowed from Jesus' side, proof to the Roman soldiers, trained in carrying out crucifixions, that Jesus was dead. Joseph of Arimathea and Nicodemus took Jesus' limp body from the cross, wrapped it and laid it in Joseph's own new tomb. Then they rolled a large stone against the entrance of the tomb and went away.

In the darkness, the silhouettes of two women can be seen opposite the grave. Mary Magdalene and the other Mary sit and stare, not believing the events that transpired in one day. Finally, they leave. **Read John 20:1–2.**

We can only imagine the shock, tears, and hushed conversations on the Sabbath following Jesus' crucifixion. After the Sabbath, on the first day of the week, Mary Magdalene, Mary the mother of James and Salome, went to Jesus' tomb. **What time of day was it?**

What did they see when they arrived at the tomb?

Mary Magdalene ran to let Peter and John know. Someone had taken Jesus, and she did not know where they laid Him. Imagine how distraught Mary Magdalene was. Her Lord had been treated in the worst of ways. Now, as far as she knows, the soldiers have taken Jesus' body from the tomb. **Read John 20:3–9.**

What did Peter and John discover when they got to the tomb?

Peter and John evidently ran ahead of Mary Magdalene. They looked in the tomb; saw that it was empty and returned to their homes. When Mary ran to tell Peter and John, the women who had stayed at the tomb had an encounter with two angels. Then the women left. Now Mary was alone at the tomb. **Read John 20:10–18.**

Nothing in our experience can compare to what these moments must have been like for Mary Magdalene. By now, you know her well. You know how far she had come from being possessed by demons to standing at the foot of the cross supporting Jesus' mother. Doubtless, she was still in shock, in unimaginable grief, and weary beyond words. **Read John 20:11. What is Mary Magdalene doing?**

Distraught, Mary was weeping and looked inside the tomb once more. **Describe what Mary saw. John 20:12**

Before she could say a word, what did the angels say to her? John 20:13

Jesus' presence was with her, but Mary did not know it. Angelic comfort resonated through the hollowness of the tomb, but Mary did not sense it. **Why was Mary heartbroken?**

Today many grope in darkness looking for God.

Mary wanted Jesus, and she did not know where to find Him. Today many grope in darkness looking for God. Loneliness and emptiness resonate through their life. Yet, if they will seek Jesus, they will find Him, even as Mary did. **What did Mary say that shows she did not understand Jesus was resurrected?**

At this time, the angels perhaps glanced at Jesus who stood behind Mary, because she turned and faced Jesus, yet she did not recognize Him. Is it any wonder? She was fatigued from the horrors of Jesus' crucifixion. Continuing to weep, her mind was not focused on the person she assumed was the gardener. She offered to take Jesus' body if the "gardener" knew where

He had been laid.

Imagine being Jesus, the Lord of the Universe, and having Mary offer to carry your body away. It is no wonder Jesus' heart was so tender toward her. **Read John 20:16. How does Jesus get Mary Magdalene's attention?**

All Jesus had to do was say Mary's name. It was not Mary Magdalene. It was plain and simple, "Mary!"

I think if there were any moment I could be present in the life of Christ, it would be this incredible moment when Mary's eyes were opened and she realized Jesus, the resurrected Christ, was standing before her. The same voice that cast demons out of her, called to her to look at Him. The recognition, love, and joy must have been out of this world! Can you imagine a deceased loved one standing before you? **Read John 20:16–17. What was Mary's response?**

Is it any wonder that Mary clung to Jesus? I would have clung to Him, too! Jesus, her Lord and King, was risen; outside the tomb, standing before her! Mary held onto Jesus until He told her to stop clinging. He explained to her that He could use her help! **Read John 20:17. First, what does Jesus tell Mary He needs to do?**

Second, the Risen Lord told Mary Magdalene that He had an assignment for her. "Anything, Lord!" we can imagine her responding. **What does Jesus want Mary to do?**

Jesus gave Mary a message to take to the others. **Read John 20:17. Write out the message Jesus told Mary to take to the others.**

Mary Magdalene represents all redeemed mankind, delivered from Satan's possession. Mary Magdalene represents what God can do with a person who is delivered out of the kingdom of darkness and transferred into God's kingdom of Light.

In the Garden of Eden, sin entered through Eve. In the Garden of the Tomb, the good news of salvation was spread through Mary Magdalene. **Read John 20:17. How does Jesus affirm the restored relationship that exists between God and man? Check one.**
❏ **I ascend to My God and Father.**
❏ **I ascend to My Father and your Father, My God and your God.**

Oh, what a majestic plan unfolded. Jesus Christ, the sacrificial Lamb, left Mary to ascend to His Father and her Father, to His God and her God! Redemption, full and complete, could never have been so sweet! **What did Mary Magdalene do?**
❏ **She hesitated.**
❏ **She acted that moment. She took off!**

Principle:
Jesus could have used an angel to proclaim the good news to the world. He chose Mary. He chose us!

The story of Mary Magdalene does not end at the empty tomb. It begins. Over the next forty days Jesus prepared His followers for His ascension and the coming of the Holy Spirit. **Read Acts 1:1–3. During the forty days between Jesus' resurrection and ascension, what did He do?**
❏ **Presented Himself alive**
❏ **Gave many convincing proofs of being alive**
❏ **Spoke about the things concerning the kingdom of God**

Jesus, once again, proclaims the kingdom of God! Imagine the attentiveness with which Mary Magdalene and the others listened! **Read Acts 1:4–5. What did Jesus command His believers to wait for in Jerusalem?**

Principle:
The Christian's effectiveness and empowerment comes from the Holy Spirit.

There was no point in the disciples attempting to do anything in Jesus' name until the Holy Spirit came upon them. It is important for us to understand that principle, also. Although we may believe in Jesus as the Son of God, believing in Jesus and the empowerment of the Holy Spirit are different.

Every believer is born of the Spirit of God. Every believer has Christ's Spirit. But not every believer lives by the filling empowerment of the Holy Spirit. Every believer has Christ's commission to be His witness. The key to empowerment and effectiveness in the kingdom of God on earth is the empowerment of the Spirit. **Read Acts 1:6–8. What did the risen Son of God explain?**

Read Acts 1:9–11. Imagine the emotion, the passion with which our Lord looked upon His loved ones and they looked upon Him this last time! He has just given them words to cling to.

The kingdom of God!

The power of the Holy Spirit on them!

Be His witnesses!

Was it in silence and awe or with shouts of praise Mary Magdalene and the others watched as Jesus ascended into the heavens and clouds? **Reread Acts 1:10. What were Jesus' followers doing?**

The key to empowerment and effectiveness in the kingdom of God on earth is the empowerment of the Spirit from above.

As they gazed intently, how good of God to send two angels to confirm what they had seen! **Where did the two angels stand?**
❏ **On a hill far away**
❏ **Beside them**

The angels stood beside them. No doubt they were there to comfort them and confirm Jesus' words. Later at Pentecost, God would send another, the Holy Spirit, who would not stand beside the disciples, but be in them! The Holy Spirit would comfort them and confirm God's words to them and glorify Christ. He would teach them, and thus Christ would be with them, and us, forever.

Apply God's Word

Where would you have been during the heat of the trial, the flogging of Jesus and Him being crucified?

Where are you now, when Jesus' morals and values, His laws and commandments, are being challenged and beaten down in our high courts?

Where would you have been when Jesus was taken and buried?

Where are you now? Do you forget about Jesus or stay close to Him in Bible study and prayer?

Up Close and Personal

What would you have done when Jesus sent you to proclaim, "He is risen!"?

What are you doing now with Jesus' command to you, "Go and make disciples of all the nations, baptizing them in the name of the Father and the Son and the Holy Spirit, teaching them to observe all that I commanded you"?

Do you pray for the daily filling and empowerment of the Holy Spirit so you can be an effective witness of God in your home, and at work, school, and church?

A Prayer Opportunity

Jesus' presence and command to go and proclaim His kingdom was not a solo command to Mary Magdalene. He chose her. He chose you. Christians are God's appointed ambassadors in the world. What is your response to Jesus' choosing and calling you?

Week Six
Thinking It Over

Please look back over your lesson and prayerfully complete the following.

1. What was most meaningful to you in your study of Mary from:

Day 1

Day 2

Day 3

Day 4

Day 5

2. How has God prompted you to increasingly invest your life in Jesus' presence and purpose as He has invested His life in you?

3. What toxins do you need to guard against in your body and spirit?

Physically

Spiritually

4. Which of Jesus' words prior to His ascension is He calling you to respond to?

5. What "golden nugget" of truth do you want to remember from this week?

6. What verse do you want to remember from this week's lesson?

7. What is the prayerful cry of your heart in relation to this week's study?

Leader's Guide

Blessings to you as you lead your group to make application of God's Word to their lives! The following has been provided as a guide for your discussion. Encourage the members to highlight or star meaningful points as they go through their daily study. Then they will be able to easily complete the Thinking It Over section each week, which will be the basis for the discussion in your group. Remember that your role as a leader is not to teach, but rather to facilitate discussion. Encourage discussion by listening and responding attentively.

Session 1: Orientation

Welcome and Introductions (15 min)
Introduce yourself and have members do the same.

Review Important Sections of the Book (15 min)
- Go over the Table of Contents and How to Get the Most Out of This Study. Call special attention to the following sections: Apply God's Word, Up Close and Personal, A Prayer Opportunity, and Thinking It Over.
- Ask members to turn to Week One, Esther, and show them where the sections you reviewed can be found. Emphasize the importance of highlighting or starring key points and meaningful applications each day.

- Direct them to Thinking It Over in Week One. Show them how easily they can complete this page if they highlight or star key points each day.
- Explain that Thinking It Over will be the basis of your discussion, so they can record anything they would like to discuss on this page. If they do not have room to write out the full thought they highlighted or starred, they can simply put the page number, and refer back to the page in the lesson.
- Explain that you will not call on them to share their prayer unless they volunteer to do so.

Session 2
Week One: Out of Control

Welcome and Brief Opening Prayer (3 min)
- Ask women to turn to Week One, Thinking It Over.
- Emphasize how much you enjoyed the week's study and are looking forward to hearing what everyone gleaned. Explain that you will watch the time and keep the group moving along.
- Review: Esther was a woman God used even though many circumstances in her life were beyond her control. Prayer and fasting preceded her bold request of King Ahasuerus, which saved the Jewish people.

Discussion Questions (25 min)
1. What was most meaningful to you as you studied Esther from:
Day 1: Out of Control?
Day 2: Choose You This Day
Day 3: The Kingdom of God
Day 4: The Three-Day Fast
Day 5: Following God's Timing

Personal Application (30 min)
2. How did God convict, stir, or prompt your heart and mind through Esther's life?
3. God used prayer and fasting in Esther's life. How might God want to use you as He did Esther, as a conduit of His grace in what appears to be a situation beyond your control?

4. What response to His Word might God want you to make as a result of studying about Esther?
5. What "golden nugget" of truth do you want to remember?
6. What verse do you want to remember from this week's study?
7. What is the prayerful cry of your heart in relation to this week's study?

Closing Prayer (2 min)

Session 3
Week 2: If God Is In Control, Why Do I Have a Headache?

Welcome and Opening Prayer (3 min)
- Ask women to turn to Week Two, Thinking It Over. Emphasize how you are looking forward to hearing from everyone.
- Review: Peter's mother-in-law was a woman who responded to Jesus' healing touch by serving Him and others.

Discussion Questions (25 min)
1. What was most meaningful to you as you studied Peter's mother-in-law from:
Day 1: Peter's Mother-in-Law
Day 2: Jesus Cares About You
Day 3: Instant Messaging…He Touched Her
Day 4: Transformed
Day 5: Transformed to Serve Jesus

Personal Application (30 min)
2. What most convicted or stirred your heart and mind this week?
3. Knowing that your health affects your ability to serve God, how is Jesus touching your heart to more responsibly eat, drink, and exercise?
4. Your lifestyle, amount of stress, response to stress, physical condition, and even a headache can affect your service to God and others. How might Jesus want to transform you? In what way do you need to better respond to Jesus' guiding touch through the Holy Spirit, prayer, and His Word?
5. What "golden nugget" of truth do you want to remember?

6. What verse do you want to remember from this week's study?
7. What is the prayerful cry of your heart in relation to this week's study?

Closing Prayer (2 min)

Session 4
Week Three: When the Dark Clouds Roll In

Welcome and Opening Prayer (3 min)
- Ask women to turn to Week Three, Thinking It Over. Comment on how you are challenged by Hannah, and emphasize that you are looking forward to hearing from everyone.
- Review: Hannah trusted God in the midst of despair and provocation. As a result, she saw God's blessings in her life.

Discussion Questions (25 min)
1. What was most meaningful to you as you studied Hannah from:
Day 1: Hannah
Day 2: When Depression Hits Home
Day 3: When Food and Words Don't Comfort
Day 4: A Woman of Honor and Excellence
Day 5: The Outcome of Faith

Personal Application (30 min)
2. How did God convict, stir, or prompt your heart and mind by Hannah's life?
3 What triggers to despair or discouragement do you need to guard against?
4. What outcome of your faith might God be trying to bring forth in the midst of your physical, emotional, financial, or other distress?
5. What "golden nugget" of truth do you want to remember?
6. What verse do you want to remember from this week's study?
7. What is the prayerful cry of your heart in relation to this week's study?

Closing Prayer (2 min)

Session 5
Week Four: When Nothing Seems to Help

Welcome and Opening Prayer (3 min)
- Ask women to turn to Week Four, Thinking It Over. Emphasize how much you enjoyed the week's study and are looking forward to hearing from everyone.
- Review: Jesus' power went forth to the woman with the issue of blood. His power can go forth in our lives also as we seek Him.

Discussion Questions (25 min)
1. What was most meaningful to you as you studied the woman with the issue of blood?
Day 1: The Woman with the Issue of Blood
Day 2: In the Midst of Suffering
Day 3: Faith and Hope Come by Hearing
Day 4: A Memorable Spiritual Moment
Day 5: Who Touched Me?

Personal Application (30 min)
2. How did God stir and prompt your heart and mind in regard to the woman with the issue of blood?
3. In what specific way does God want you to take care of your health, knowing that one day someone may take care of you?
4. How is this lesson calling you to speak of your faith so others in dire situations can hear the good news of Christ's power?
5. What "golden nugget" of truth do you want to remember?
6. What verse do you want to remember from this week's study?
7. What is the prayerful cry of your heart in relation to this week's study?

Closing Prayer (2 min)

Session 6
Week Five: A Diseased Heart

Welcome and Opening Prayer (3 min)
- Ask women to turn to Week Five, Thinking It Over. Comment on how convicting this week's study was and how you are looking forward to hearing from everyone.
- Review: Jesus loved Martha. His love led Him to confront her about being busy and bothered by things. He called her to faith and to choose the good part of life.

Discussion Questions (25 min)
1. What was most meaningful to you as you studied Martha from:
Day 1: Martha
Day 2: So God May Be Glorified
Day 3: Do You Believe?
Day 4: Lazarus, Come Forth!
Day 5: Passion or Profession?

Personal Application (30 min)
2. How did God speak to your heart as you studied Martha's life?
3. In what way does this lesson stimulate you to move beyond being a woman who only professes her faith to being a woman of passion?
4. How is God challenging you to keep your heart healthy physically and spiritually?
5. What "golden nugget" of truth do you want to remember?
6. What verse do you want to remember from this week's study?
7. What is the prayerful cry of your heart in relation to this week's study?

Closing Prayer (2 min)

Session 7
Week Six: He Saw the Pure Me

Welcome and Opening Prayer (3 min)
- Ask women to turn to Week Six, Thinking It Over. Emphasize how touched you were by this week's study and how you are looking forward to hearing from everyone.
- Review: Mary Magdalene models extravagant love and how Jesus desires for our body and soul be cleansed of any stronghold.

Discussion Questions (25 min)
1. What was most meaningful to you as you studied Mary Magdalene from:
Day 1: Mary Magdalene
Day 2: Delivered Into God's Kingdom
Day 3: Mary Chose Jesus' Presence and Purpose
Day 4: Mary Magdalene Shared Jesus' Passion
Day 5: He Is Risen

Personal Application (30 min)
2. How has God prompted you to increasingly invest your life in Jesus' presence and purpose as He has invested His life in you?
3. What toxins do you need to guard against in your body and spirit physically and spiritually?
4. Which of Jesus' words prior to His ascension is He calling you to respond to?
5. What "golden nugget" of truth do you want to remember?
6. What verse do you want to remember from this week's study?
7. What is the prayerful cry of your heart in relation to this week's study?

Closing Prayer (2 min)